After Mi      ꞁ

Marilyn J. Bardsley

"Gracie," Bonaventure Cemetery

Electronic edition published 2013 by RosettaBooks, LLC, New
York.
Cover photo by C. Elliott Bardsley and jacket design by Misha
Beletsky
ISBN Print-on-demand edition: 9780795333453

Contents

Acknowledgments

This ebook and the entire Crimescape series of short nonfiction crime ebooks would not exist without the encouragement and marketing efforts of Arthur Klebanoff, the CEO of Rosetta Books, and his highly professional team. My special thanks go to Rosetta's Greg Freed for guidance in developing Crimescape's cover art and for ensuring the manuscripts' safe passage through the publishing process. Special thanks also go to Tracy Majka for her dedicated and critical reading of Crimescape manuscripts, and her counsel on style and editing.

I am very much indebted to Frank "Sonny" Seiler, lead defense attorney for three of the Jim Williams' trials, for sharing with me his views on the case, and facilitating access to trial transcripts and other key documents. I am also very grateful to Spencer Lawton Jr., the former Chatham County District Attorney for 28 years. Lawton led the prosecution of Jim Williams in all four trials. He was kind enough to provide me with internal documents he created on the prosecution's strategy and case theory, along with permission to share them with our readers.

The hours I spent with Joe and Nancy Goodman, both longtime friends of Jim Williams, helped me greatly to understand Williams' character. Joe was his closest and most trusted friend for more than three decades. Jim was like a father to him, and he never forgot it. My talks with Carol Freeman brought to life the wild and entertaining side of Williams' personality.

I cannot forget Jeanne Papy, who let me use the excellent photos she took of Mercer House parties and some of the actors in the "Midnight" movie. She is in the photo at the bottom of this section in the dress she wore for the filming.

Jeanne Papy at Mercer House Party
Courtesy of Photographer

I must also thank Ulla Jensen, who accompanied me to many of the interviews, and veteran Savannah reporter Jan Skutch, who gave insight on the people I needed to interview.

I want to express my thanks to the more than 50 people who shared their stories with me over the years: Judge Michael Barker, Diane Silver Berryhill, Miriam K. Center, Dawn Dupree, John Duncan, Alison (Ali) Fennell, Michael Hawk, Nancy Heffernan, Mykell Holdren, Dennis Miller, Ruby Mooney, Joel Moore, David Sands, Randy Shuman, Kenneth Worthy II, Alex Raskin, Esther Shaver, and many individuals who chose to remain anonymous.

www.crimescape.com

Chapter 1

Good and Evil

A decade ago, I abandoned manic, impersonal Washington, D.C., and escaped to the quiet calm of semitropical Savannah. As the executive editor of Court TV's Crime Library website, I had the luxury of working anywhere with a good Internet and cell phone connection.

Forsyth Park

Savannah is a truly lovely city where atmosphere hangs as heavy as the Spanish moss on the giant live oak trees. The elegant, seductively beautiful historic district, with its spacious porches, walled gardens and intricate ironwork, is a glimpse of a treasured past, now lovingly restored. Traveling around the historic downtown, one encounters a shady square with gardens and monuments every few blocks. But the city is so much more than an antebellum grand dame. It is a unique state of mind:

discreetly scandalous, insular, stubbornly resistant to change, and resplendent with eccentric charm and perfect manners.

Rosemary Daniell, a prominent Savannah writer, aptly described the special character of her city: "Despite this city's pastel beauty, it also has a dark underside. Within its hothouse atmosphere, the present runs concurrently with the past; events that happened decades before are discussed as though they happened yesterday, including a number of scenes of sex and violence extreme enough to rival any dreamed up by Tennessee Williams."

After a few months, I found myself fascinated by Jim Williams, one of Savannah's most memorable characters. Like many others, I had read John Berendt's *Midnight in the Garden of Good and Evil*, and watched Clint Eastwood's movie, starring Kevin Spacey as Jim Williams and Jude Law as Danny Hansford, the lover that Williams shot.

As the publisher of more than 700 Crime Library stories, I found the case unique. Jim Williams spent the better part of a decade and more than a million dollars defending himself in four separate murder trials, punctuated by a two-year stint in a substandard county jail.

To get to the heart of the Williams case, I began a series of some 50-plus interviews: socially prominent Savannah "bluebloods," antique dealers, drag queens, hairdressers, attorneys, bartenders, and others who rubbed elbows with Jim Williams and Danny Hansford.

What emerged is the story of a charismatic man with astonishing talents to whom the city of Savannah owes an enormous debt. Jim Williams was a highly talented artist and entrepreneur who saved many of the grand old houses of Savannah from the wrecking ball. However, I unexpectedly found a man who indulged in clearly unethical and illegal activities that could have put him behind bars well before he shot Danny Hansford. Jim was often an arrogant man with a surprising predatory streak, who had no qualms about exploiting people at any level of society.

Ironically, the intersection of these conflicting currents in Jim Williams' personality gave birth to his greatest contributions to Savannah: The notoriety of Danny Hansford's shooting and the four trials, John Berendt's book, and Clint Eastwood's movie put Savannah squarely on the tourist circuit, generating millions of dollars of revenue, which flowed into the city for more than a decade and, most likely, will continue to do so well into the future.

I invite you to come along with me into the very complicated world of Jim Williams, but first, let's take a look at the influences that shaped the character of this man.

www.crimescape.com

Chapter 2

Most Likely to Succeed

Some have characterized Jim Williams' life as a Horatio Alger story. Not so, said Kenneth Worthy II, an antiques dealer and friend of Williams. According to Worthy, Jim's parents were never poor. They weren't cash-rich, but they were quality people with decades of good breeding. Jim personally enjoyed researching and writing about his family's English heritage and its journey in the New World from Boston to central Georgia. They were a family of prosperous farmers.

James Arthur Williams was born December 11, 1930, in Gordon, a small mining and farming town east of Macon in rural Georgia. His father, Arthur Williams, was a barber and his mother, Blanche Brooks Williams, was a secretary for a local kaolin mining company. Jim's thick dark hair and good looks were a gift from his rakishly handsome father. He had one sibling, a younger sister, Dorothy, whom he nicknamed D.O., which was short for Dorothy Ollie.

In 1983, Jim wrote fondly about an idyllic childhood in a close-knit family of grandparents, uncles and aunts, who frequently got together at his grandparents' farm at Turkey Creek, some 18 miles from Gordon. Ultimately, his father and mother divorced and his father remarried, but his father and his new wife lived in close proximity to the children. A number of Jim's writings about the history of his family, his early interest in saving disappearing Georgia architecture, and stories about restoring homes in Savannah and South Carolina are captured in *Savannah's Jim Williams and His Southern Houses* by his sister, Dr. Dorothy Williams Kingery.

Gordon, GA

The entrepreneurial spirit was strong in Jim as a youngster. Worthy told me that even at the age of 14, Jim was buying and selling antiques he thought were valuable or could expand his knowledge. Jim's strong business sense and work ethic so impressed his school principal that once he let the teenager out of school to close a transaction. To encourage Jim's love of wooden furniture, his father built him a wood shop, which is still standing in an old tobacco barn, according to Worthy.

From his youth onward, Jim had a deep love and respect for history and its survivors, antique pottery, and furniture. It greatly pained him to see the destruction of so many fine old rural houses as enormous areas were cleared to plant pine trees for the pulp and paper industry. Later, this early fascination with history expanded beyond what he saw and found in central Georgia, even beyond colonial America, to the antique treasures of Europe and Asia that he would ultimately possess.

First, he had to go to college to get the credentials he needed to become a credible architectural preservationist. With the help of his mother's salary, he enrolled at the Ringling College of Art and Design in Sarasota, Florida, to study interior design. At the same time, he studied antiques, architecture, and old houses.

While at school, he also studied piano and organ. The normal program for an interior design certificate was three years, but he only attended for two, from August 1948 to May 1950. After art school, Jim studied at Mercer University in Macon, Georgia. Then he went to work with an interior design company in New Orleans, He was even in the Air Force for a short time before he settled in Savannah.

www.crimescape.com

Chapter 3

Overcoming Obstacles

In 1946, Britain's Lady Nancy Astor said during her visit, "Savannah was a beautiful lady with a dirty face." Her comment shamed Savannah, but not enough to do anything about it. Preston Russell and Barbara Hines summed up the problem in their history of the city: "Prominent businessmen who cared nothing for old architecture assumed there was little to save."

In 1952, Jim left the Air Force and decided to stay in Savannah during a time of economic growth and pride in America's future. He fell in love with the city and the architecture, and was greatly disturbed at the loss of houses in the historic district, which were destroyed to make way for parking lots and garages. It seemed like every week, another house in the historic or Victorian district was torn down. Ironically, the value of the old Savannah gray bricks as building construction material was often greater than the value of the house, so some houses were torn down just so the bricks could be sold.

To make ends meet, Jim became a salesman for Klug's Furniture Company at the corner of Victory Drive and Abercorn Street. For a while, Jim invested his time and impressive knowledge of art and antiques in a joint venture with his friend Jack Kieffer. Kieffer put up the money and Jim put up the expertise, but the venture did not survive. Even though Kieffer remained a lifelong friend, Jim told close associates that Kieffer made out much better financially in the venture than he did.

Jim's dream was to restore important historic homes in Savannah. What was going on in downtown Savannah was happening to cities everywhere in the country. The inner city had become crime-infested, and affluent people moved out to the suburbs, leaving lovely large homes to fall into disrepair. These homes in the historic and adjacent Victorian districts became tenements rented to multiple large families, which further accelerated the decline in property values. Wealthy families built their mansions in suburban Ardsley Park. Two decades later, as executives from northern states with harsh winter climates planned their retirements, many of them were enticed by the gated country club communities on Skidaway Island, like the Landings, rather than settling in a city that was still in decay.

The early 1950s was a watershed time for the city. The Georgia legislature gave the city permission to raze the historic City Market, which was replaced by an ugly parking garage. Finally, the people of Savannah woke up, and although they couldn't save the old City Market, an influential group created the Historic Savannah Foundation in 1955. As one foundation member explained, "We needed one crisis, one central issue that would focus attention on the downtown area. This happened to be it."

The decline of Savannah's historic district worsened in the 1960s as suburban shopping centers and Oglethorpe Mall, Savannah's first shopping mall, made it unnecessary to go downtown. Savannah's banks, like banks all over the country that faced a deteriorating inner city, redlined the area. In other words, they would not lend money for restoration projects. Downtown property values plunged, and large stately homes in the downtown and midtown districts could be purchased for less than $5,000.

For a man like Jim Williams, brilliant, ambitious, and absolutely hell-bent on becoming a major force in restoring Savannah's architectural jewels, the funding problem was very challenging. The wealthy families of Savannah and the city's financial institutions were extremely hesitant to invest any money in risky downtown restoration ventures. The fledgling historical foundation was a good start, but it wasn't going to further the dreams of Jim Williams anytime soon.

Ever the businessman and opportunist, he came up with an ingenious—but unethical and ultimately illegal—solution to the problem of getting his restoration projects funded and increasing his friendships with important people. Jim was a very masculine gay man with a trim body, a handsome face, thick dark hair, and penetrating dark eyes. Moreover, he was extremely intelligent, poised, an expert in antiques and architectural design, and blessed with exquisite taste. Jim was remarkably persuasive and struck most people as being extremely trustworthy. In short, he was one attractive and desirable bachelor.

Jim quickly learned that a number of wealthy and influential gay and bisexual men were locked into the married life that Savannah society required its upper crust to embrace. Some of these men were at the top of important financial institutions and businesses that would ultimately determine whether or not there would be funding in the future to restore historic Savannah.

Jim understood the conundrum that these men faced. They may have dreamed about young gay boys as sexual partners, but the risk of seeking out such relationships was fraught with risks. Yes, many young male hustlers hung around the Bull Street squares, but engaging them was far too dangerous. There was great potential for scandal, extortion, blackmail, and even personal injury if these men engaged in homosexual relationships. As a very cultured, handsome man with enormous charisma and persuasive abilities, developing sexual relationships with influential gay men was not difficult for him. Jim represented a "safe" relationship for men whose married life and reputation demanded the utmost discretion.

To a businessman like Jim, the conundrum for these men represented an opportunity to insinuate himself into Savannah's old-money crowd and coax his new influential friends to fund his restoration projects. He cultivated the spouses of his new male friends with his knowledge of interior design to charm his way into Savannah's high society.

Jim didn't work this avenue solely with his own charms. Some of his gay married friends longed for sexual partners much younger than Jim, but could not afford to be seen cruising gay bars or making sexual overtures to employees or acquaintances. Opportunist that he was, Jim found a way to serve the needs of his friends. Unfortunately, the service Jim provided—which I stumbled upon early in my research—was immoral and very illegal.

I was having some painting and wallpapering done at our home when Buddy, our wallpaper guru, overheard me talking about Jim Williams.

"My mother hated him," he blurted out. "She was the manager of the Burger King at the bus station back then."

Greyhound bus station, Savannah

My thoughts focused on the downtown Greyhound bus station. There was only one in Savannah.

"She'd watch him [Jim] as the buses came in from rural Georgia and South Carolina," Buddy continued. "He'd look over the teenagers coming off the buses and go talk to the good-looking ones."

"Then what did he do?" I said.

Buddy shrugged. "My mother saw him walk away with the boy he chose, but she didn't know where they went." He paused for a moment. "She knew what guys like that were up to. You see that kind of thing when you work at the bus station. He didn't do that once or twice. He was around a lot, looking for runaways."

Seeing Jim month after month checking out boys in their mid-teens and often leaving the station with them disgusted her. She assumed that he befriended the boys for his own pleasure, and that was partly true. Jim loved sex with young men and boys.

What she didn't know was that Williams also vetted the kids back at his house. If they had left their small town because they were gay or were desperate enough to make some money satisfying Jim's friends, he kept them around for awhile to make sure that they weren't a liability. Once he decided they were reliable, Jim would introduce them to his friends.

Later, when he was much more successful, Jim didn't have to hang around the bus station looking for young talent for himself or his friends. All he had to do was to go out into the squares around Bull Street and persuade some of the teenagers to come to home with him. He got to know which ones he could trust.

Confirming this aspect of Jim's character was very challenging. Although many in the gay community knew what Jim was doing, locating victims who would agree to an interview was difficult. Many of the boys that Jim had exploited were dead from AIDS, drugs, or urban violence, but eventually, I was able to interview two who are still around. One is a hairdresser and the other is a performer. Jim would invite them to his fabulous Mercer House for a drink. They were 15 or 16 years old, poor, absolutely awed by the opulence of the house, and desperate for money.

Oglethorpe Club, Savannah

It is unlikely that Jim procured boys for wealthy clients for money. What Jim sought in exchange was influence. He needed acceptance into a level of society that normally would have been closed to him because he was not from a distinguished old Savannah family, nor was he from "old money." Gradually, because he was helpful, charming, and did not appear gay, Jim was able to use his interior design expertise, knowledge of antiques, and discreet sexual services to insinuate himself into the upper reaches of Savannah society. Savannah is very tolerant of sin in the rarified reaches of society, as long as it doesn't become the subject of conversation at the exclusive Oglethorpe Club.

www.crimescape.com

Chapter 4

Lean Times

One can most accurately characterize Jim Williams' early years in Savannah as very lean. He had only one suit to his name and frequently borrowed money for routine expenses. His longtime friend, Joe Goodman, met Jim when he was just 11 years old. They were both living around Washington Square in downtown Savannah. Jim was 18 years older than Joe and became like a father figure to him. Joe's father was a merchant marine and frequently worked away from home. Jim was on a subsistence budget, so Joe's mother frequently fed Jim, as did the Saseen girls who belonged to the Saseen Bonding Company family in Savannah. Joe explained that Jim was broke for quite a long time in those early years. He bought a lot on credit and borrowed frequently.

Jim began restoring homes in 1955, when he bought three row houses on East Congress Street for very little money. Eventually he bought the whole block, rented the houses, and then sold them for a reasonable profit. Joe remembers those times vividly. Jim built his young restoration work crew from Joe and his friends that lived around Washington Square, paying them when he could.

"Want to start making some money?" Jim boomed as he enthusiastically rounded up the boys in the neighborhood. They did things like tearing down walls and putting in new plaster. They all liked him and never suspected he was gay.

Once he pocketed some money from the Congress Street restorations and rentals, Jim set his sights on the houses on nearby East St. Julian. He would put small down payments on houses to hold them until he had the funding to start work. He was not making a lot of money, but he did make an important friend, Henry Dunn, the head of Georgia State Savings Association, who funded a number of Jim's restorations.

Row houses on E. Congress St.

The first house on East Julian Street that Jim set his eyes on was the Odingsells House, which was the first house of the multi-talented South Carolina native Major Charles Odingsells. Odingsells fought in the Revolutionary War, became a prosperous planter on Skidaway Island and the owner of Little Wassaw Island.

Often, Jim would live in a house after it was restored until it could be sold. In 1961, when he finished the restoration, he moved in and brought his antique shop with him.

The next major restoration was the Hampton Lillibridge house on East Bryan Street. Originally, the house was going to be moved, along with another house, to Washington Square, to become the headquarters of the Port Society. During the move, one of the houses collapsed. The Historic Savannah Foundation let Jim buy and take over the restoration of the remaining Lillibridge house.

Jim moved the house across the street from his home on East St. Julian and eventually bought the whole block.

Jim Williams, 1963
Copyright Savannah Morning News

www.crimescape.com

Chapter 5

Things That Go Bump in the Night

The Bird Girl
Photo by Jeanne Papy

Jim Williams was very superstitious and interested in knowing the future. Some said that he had a deep belief in magic and the spirit world. For those who read John Berendt's book or saw Clint Eastwood's movie, one of the most interesting characters was a colorful voodoo princess called Minerva, a pseudonym for Valerie Fennel Aiken Boles, who lived in Beaufort, South Carolina. She seemed almost omnipresent, casting spells on District Attorney Spencer Lawton, witnesses, and jurors. She also performed rites to appease the spirit of Danny Hansford, whom she reasonably assumed was angry about being shot. Boles learned her skills from her husband M.J. Washington, who called himself "Dr. Eagle." Jim was a client of Dr. Eagle, and when he died, Jim used Boles, who took over his practice as a "root doctor."

Sonny Seiler and "Minerva"
(portrait)

According to a man who frequented the Monterey Square area where Jim's Mercer House is located, Boles was in Savannah frequently in the 1970s and 1980s, finding a ready market for her services from Jim and others. She passed away in early May 2009. Her age was undisclosed.

Root doctors are still a big thing in the Low Country, especially in parts of South Carolina. They claim to perform a wide range of personal services, such as getting revenge on an enemy, removing curses, preparing love potions, or even ensuring a criminal a shorter prison sentence. They are a current-day version of a shaman or witch doctor using herbs and potions to perform their magic rites.

In addition to using Boles' services, Joe Goodman said that Jim often went to palm readers, even on one of his trips to Europe where Joe accompanied him. In many ways, it is not surprising that Jim had a deep belief in the spirit world, considering what he went through when he renovated and later lived in the Hampton Lillibridge house.

Hampton Lillibridge House

According to James Caskey in *Haunted Savannah*, in 1799, Rhode Islander Hampton Lillibridge built the three-story New England-style house with a gambrel roof and unusual widow's walk, near the center of Savannah. Lillibridge also had a plantation on Sea Island, which is now a resort community with the high-end Cloister boutique hotel, south of Savannah. Jim bought the house in 1963, and moved it to 507 East St. Julian Street, across from the Odingsells house that Jim had restored.

The brick masons working on the house complained about the noise of people running around on the upper floor, but there were no steps to the upper floor at that time and no evidence that anyone human was up there. Throughout the restoration, the masons threatened to quit working on the house because they heard loud voices, furniture being moved around, and feet stomping on the upper floor.

Jim, Joe Goodman, and a number of other people also heard sounds that couldn't be explained by any natural means. Joe, who does not believe in the supernatural, said he heard heavy chains being dragged across the floor above when there was no one on that floor.

Another time, Joe and Jim were standing outside of the house. Joe saw a Siamese cat looking at them from the upper floor window.

"Williams," he said, pointing to the cat. "Look up there. That's Nooney."

"Sure enough," Jim admitted after staring hard at the cat. "It's Nooney." Nooney, Jim's cat, had died two years earlier.

One of the most chilling episodes in the house occurred later, when Jim was out of town and three of his friends tried to persuade the masons to go back to work in the house. The friends heard noises that sounded like people upstairs, even though the house was empty. One of the friends went up to investigate. Margaret Wayt DeBolt describes the event in *Savannah Spectres and Other Strange Tales*:

"When the others went looking for him, they were shocked to find him lying face down on the floor. He said he felt as though he had just walked into a pool of cold water, and was being overpowered by some force. He had dropped to the floor to try to avoid whatever seemed to be drawing him toward the thirty-foot drop of the unfinished chimney shaft."

Various other specters were seen at the windows, including a dark-haired man in a suit and a bow tie. Another time, a gray-haired man with a gray suit and white tie was seen when the house was vacant and locked.

It's really no wonder that Jim personally believed the place was haunted. Once, when he was talking to a police officer in the house, they heard a crashing sound from a room in which Williams had a pipe organ. When the policeman went upstairs, the pipe organ was fine. Nothing could have made the repeated loud crashing noises. At other times, when Jim was in bed, he heard footsteps come into his room and stop at the foot of his bed.

The house developed a reputation. One night, when Jim was in Europe buying antiques, neighbors heard singing. Through the lighted windows, they could see figures dancing. However, the neighbors found out the next day that the house was empty and locked.

Jim had spent a great deal of time and money painstakingly restoring the house and had no desire to see it lose its value because of supernatural forces. To fix the problem, he contacted the Right Reverend Albert R. Stewart, an Episcopal bishop, to perform the rite of exorcism in December 1963. Joe Goodman was there when the bishop came to the house, fully robed with young acolytes. Joe recalled that the bishop said a few words and blessed the house, but the ceremony, which was reported to have lasted 45 minutes, was really not much more than 10 to 15 minutes. Perhaps if the exorcism rite had been longer, the effects would have been more lasting. The spirits kept away for about ten days, but then returned.

The Hampton Lillibridge house was so obviously haunted that various psychics came to investigate both the phenomena and the history of the house. While the house was being moved from its original location on East Bryan Street, a workman died when the house that was being moved with it collapsed. Some believed that a sailor who once lived in the house had committed suicide by hanging himself in one of the upstairs bedrooms. Jim later recalled that when the house was moved, there was an old crypt on the lot underneath the house, but no one thought to investigate it then. By the time Jim thought of checking out the crypt, it had already been covered up.

As time went on, Jim's charismatic personality, expertise in antiques, and dedication to furthering the preservation of homes in the historic district earned him a growing number of friends in Savannah's old-money class. He was also making inroads with influential bankers like Mills B. Lane Jr. Lane was the head of Citizens and Southern National Bank, the largest bank in the South, and a major force in Georgia politics. When Lane returned from Atlanta to live in Savannah, the city of his birth, Jim sold him a lot across the street from his house on St. Julien. Good neighbors and friends for years, they used to walk around the neighborhood drinking wine and talking about the restoration of downtown Savannah.

Eventually, Jim sold the Hampton Lillibridge house, despite its notoriety, or perhaps because of it. Subsequent owners of the house have reported a number of strange events, like hearing inexplicable music or furniture moved around in empty rooms on the floor above, but the ghostly events did not have the frequency or intensity that had existed when Jim owned it. Most of the unusual happenings were experienced by people who did not live in the house.

www.crimescape.com

Chapter 6

The Gods Smiled

Until the mid-1960s, things were tight financially for Jim. The profit margins on sales of restorations and antiques were insufficient for Jim's driving ambition. He would take his earnings and put small down payments on a number of properties, hoping that he would be able to eventually earn enough to buy them outright or get enough in loans to secure them.

At one point, Jim found an extra $5,000 to buy Cabbage Island, just below Wilmington Island in Wassau Sound on the Georgia coast, where he and his friends could drink, fish, and party. Little did he know what this dubious piece of vacation real estate would do for his fortunes. Cabbage Island is a large marsh island with very little land mass and is virtually under six feet of water at high tide.

In an extraordinary bit of luck, he made a small fortune selling the island to the Kerr-McGee Corporation, that wanted to develop the large phosphate deposits on the island. Kerr-McGee bought the island from Jim in 1966 for $660,000. In 1968, Kerr-McGee also purchased nearby Little Tybee Island for the same purpose as Cabbage Island two years earlier. When Kerr-McGee petitioned the state for a permit to strip mine phosphates from deposits 40 feet below the marsh surfaces, there was a public outcry and the state passed a law protecting all Georgia tidal marshes from strip mining.

Jim's sudden treasure was a watershed moment in his career. It was an enormous jumpstart to his ability to invest in important properties, lavish restorations, high-value antiques, and collectable treasures. Now he had the means to go over to Europe several times a year and purchase British and European antiques at excellent prices that he could mark up substantially when he sold them to customers in the U.S. He would attend auctions at Christie's, Sotheby's and other auction houses to buy for antiques for his business, as well as for his personal collection of Fabergé.

Jim explained to Joe, who now worked for Jim doing odd jobs, how he was able to get such valuable antiques overseas. As socialism became entrenched in Europe and the U.K., taxes on the wealthy were increased to confiscatory levels, especially inheritance taxes, to pay for the social welfare state. Rather than make it publicly known that they had to sell valuable antiques to pay their taxes, wealthy families concluded transactions with Jim that ensured confidentiality for the sellers. Joe said that he would get an exclusive arrangement on a house that was being sold to pay "death taxes" and then buy all the furniture in the house at a bargain price. He would then ship over only the most valuable antiques to his shop in Savannah and arrange for sale of the less valuable pieces in country. Other bargains could be found as formerly wealthy citizens of Russia and other Eastern European countries were forced to flee and live on whatever treasures they were able to take with them.

In quick succession, Jim was able to secure and restore some of the most important historic houses and buildings in Savannah.

First was Armstrong House, an opulent palazzo with an exterior in the Italian Renaissance style on Bull Street near Forsyth Park. It was built for George Ferguson Armstrong, his wife, Lucy, and a daughter. Armstrong's Strachan Shipping Company had made him a substantial fortune. Construction was finally completed after several years in 1919 at the then-astronomical sum of $680,000, or so goes the legend.

Armstrong's widow eventually donated the exquisite property to Armstrong Junior College. The house remained a college for the next three decades until it was acquired by the Historic Savannah Foundation in 1966, when the growth of the school required a move to a larger location. Over time, Armstrong Junior College expanded greatly and became Armstrong University, a state university.

Armstrong House

Jim bought Armstrong House from the Historic Savannah Foundation in 1967 and moved his antique shop there for a couple of years. The house was in excellent shape and did not need restoration. In 1970, Jim sold it to the law firm of Bouhan, Williams & Levy. One of the law firm's senior partners is Frank W. "Sonny" Seiler, who breeds the famous Uga bulldog mascots for the University of Georgia.

For those who have seen the *Midnight* movie, the early scene between writer John Kelso and the actor who played Williams' attorney was filmed inside the magnificent Armstrong House. Jim's real attorney, Sonny Seiler, appeared in the movie as Judge White.

Jim's next project was the Pink House in 1968. The Georgian home was made of red bricks and then covered with white plaster. However, the color of the bricks kept bleeding through the plaster and white paint, creating a pink house. No matter how many times the house was painted white, it eventually turned pink again. Finally one of the owners gave up and painted the exterior pink.

The Pink House

The pink mansion on Reynolds Square was built by James Habersham Jr., who was from one of Savannah's founding families. It was saved from demolition by Alida Harper Fowlkes, who bought it and turned it into a tea room. Later, the Georgian Tea Room closed and the house fell into a serious state of dilapidation—that is, until Jim undertook its restoration. After a contentious time with the city government on granting a liquor license, Jim finally sold the building, which was turned into a popular Savannah restaurant called The Olde Pink House.

All of this was a warm-up for the pinnacle of his restorations, his personal residence, the now-famous Mercer House.

Chapter 7

Jim's Gay Savannah

"Savannah, like New York, had its own queer counterculture," blogger Jack Miller wrote. "The community was much smaller than New York, but in proportion to the population of Savannah, just as essential to the city's society, if not more so... Savannah was arguably more tolerant of gays than New York..."

Herb Traub Jr.
(portrait)

In the late 1960s and early 1970s, Jim would go out for drinks at the Pirate's Cove, a bar next door to the Pirate's House restaurant that was frequented by gays and was owned by Herb Traub Jr. The bartender at the Pirate's Cove was Bill Durden, who then started up what became a busy bar called the Lamp Post on East Bay Street. The Lamp Post was popular with gays and cross-dressers as well as prostitutes who came in with their customers. Jim did not try to hide his sexual orientation to his close friends, like Carol Freeman. In fact, she accompanied him at least once on his visits to the Lamp Post as a lark.

Miriam K. Center, a writer friend of Jim's, described the 1970s as Savannah's "sexual coming of age." Jim, she told me, loved "street trash" and frequented the bars looking for wild young things. A number of gay bars sprung up in that era, like Dr. Feelgood's on Drayton, the Basement on Bull Street, Woody's on River Street, and Faces on Lincoln, all of which are closed.

In the last half of that decade, a straight couple opened a three-story disco nightclub called Who's Who at Bay and Abercorn. It was a mixed crowd of people 18-40 with gays making up approximately 75% of the clientele. The club had female impersonators like Lady Chablis and was the largest dance club in the city. Eventually, the owners opened up a bar on the other side called The Fountain, where the famous singer Emma Kelly performed. The bar burned down just before Hurricane Hugo hit the Low Country in 1989.

Jim often came to Who's Who in the afternoon and played backgammon with his friends. Once, Danny Hansford came into the bar, high on booze or marijuana, and quickly got loud and obnoxious with Jim. After that, Danny was not allowed in the bar.

A friend of Jim's who frequented Who's Who told me that when Jim spotted an attractive young man, he'd ask the bartenders to find out if the young man would be receptive to having drinks with Jim. That way, Jim would not have to face rejection if the young man was not interested. Jim had a big problem with rejection—one that this friend personally experienced. He explained that while Jim had always been a gentleman to him, he lost his temper when he turned Jim down sexually. This particular friend had a significant other to whom he was faithful.

"What's wrong with me?" Jim yelled and grabbed the friend's arm. "What can a Jew boy do for you that I can't do for you?" Later, Jim apologized to his friend, but the episode was not easily forgotten.

A nightclub that Jim frequented was Club One on Jefferson Street, which still showcases female impersonators like the Lady Chablis. Club One is similar to Who's Who, but larger. Jim became friends with bartender Ali Fennell when he dropped in late evenings for his vodka and tonic with a twist of lime. The Lady Chablis also performed at a popular bar on Congress Street called the Pick-up.

The Lady Chablis
Photo by Jeanne Papy

Another aspect of Jim's gay Savannah were the bachelor parties he would have for his gay friends, many of whom were designers, decorators, and antique dealers from the Savannah, Hilton Head, and Charleston areas. Once Jim moved into Mercer House, he had a black-tie Christmas party for the bachelors that was held the day after the Christmas party for the socialites. He supposedly discontinued this tradition after the death of Danny Hansford.

I heard about other parties when I interviewed Mike Hawk several years ago. He told me about the smaller Sunday parties. It was illegal to buy alcohol in stores on Sunday. Restaurants even needed special licenses to offer drinks, and could only offer them after church was over at 12:30 p.m. Jim's solution to this problem was to have his gay friends in for drinks and conversation.

www.crimescape.com

Chapter 8

The High Life

In the 1970s, Jim's many years of hard work started to pay off. Mercer House, purchased in 1969, had been transformed into an aristocratic showplace. His antiques business was thriving, and—perhaps most importantly—his place in Savannah society continued to rise.

Of the scores of homes Jim restored during his career, Mercer House at 429 Bull Street was his greatest triumph. Ironically, Mercer House was never the home of any members of the Mercer family, including songwriter Johnny Mercer. Construction of General Hugh W. Mercer's house was started in 1860, but was not completed until almost 10 years later. The house had various owners over the years. At one time, it was the home of the Savannah Shriners Alee Temple.

In 1967, the Historic Savannah Foundation bought the house to prevent it from being torn down. The property, which included the main house, a carriage house and gardens, took up the entire block from Bull Street on Monterey Square to Whitaker between West Gordon and West Wayne. Two years later, Jim bought the house, which was in unfortunate shape, but still structurally sound, and spent the next two years restoring it. In the upstairs ballroom, Jim installed the huge pipe organ that he had bought years earlier from the Masonic temple. The basement became the workshop for Jim's antique restoration business. Under the management of gifted artist and shopkeeper Barry Thomas, Jim's craftsmen restored the fruits of his frequent antiques-buying trips abroad.

Mercer House at Christmas
Photo by Jeanne Papy

According to Jim's friend Joe Goodman, the antiques business was much more profitable than restoring historic homes. His best clients were from out of town: DuPonts, Rockefellers, and Kemper Insurance executives. Over time, he had built up such an exclusive group of antiques buyers that he only opened the house and shop for wealthy clients who flew in on buying expeditions. For example, Jim would buy prestigious items like Napoleon's carriage crest, Chinese porcelain, Flemish tapestries, a leather desk folio made for Czar Nicholas II, and elaborate treasures that the House of Fabergé had crafted for the Russian czars.

Joe was at Mercer House when Jacqueline Onassis visited with her friend Maurice Tempelsman. Jim said Jackie had offered $90,000 for a small green jade Fabergé box that was encrusted with rubies and diamonds, but he told Joe he had refused to sell it to her. Jim had just paid $70,000 for it at a Christie's auction in Europe.

Sonny Seiler, Jim's attorney, described how Jim made a small fortune by importing English furniture from the Caribbean island of Grenada, a former British colony. He was looking for four-poster beds and asked a local man where to find them. "Up the mountain," he said. "Where the blacks live." As the British abandoned the politically volatile island, they left their antique furniture behind. Jim and his local guide took a station wagon up the mountain and parked in front of the shanties. They negotiated for the four-poster beds and Jim paid cash on the spot. It was a good price for the locals, and a good investment for Jim.

Jim made several trips to Grenada and stayed a few days on each trip, taking load after load of furniture that would be shipped to Savannah. Some of the antique hand-carved four-poster beds had a unique nutmeg design. Even though the furniture was in poor shape, Jim's workshop was able to restore it. One bed and nightstand that Jim bought for a couple hundred dollars sold for $27,000.

The story of Mercer House and its treasures is inextricably wound up in the famous Christmas parties Jim gave. Usually, Jim hosted two parties: One for the doctors, lawyers, merchant chiefs and society friends, and one for Jim's bachelor friends, including antiques dealers and other design professionals, salon owners and various gay and bisexual friends. They were elaborate affairs with excellent Low Country food and drinks, gorgeous flower arrangements, engaging entertainment and perfect southern hospitality. These parties were the big Savannah social events of the year.

One courthouse insider told me an amusing story, but I can't vouch for its veracity: The late Judge Lionel Drew Jr. was invited to one of Jim's Christmas parties, but he showed up on the wrong night—the night of the bachelor party. Allegedly, Jim answered the door in drag and calmly told Judge Drew that his party had taken place the previous night.

Jim traveled in luxurious style when he went abroad. Joe went with Jim on one of his trips to London, and then to Geneva for a Fabergé auction. They flew first class and stayed at the Ritz. Jim had a lot of friends in Europe. At night, they would be picked up in a Bentley and driven to the exclusive Crockfords Club, where they could gamble in a casino upstairs.

Crockfords Club, London
Photo by Debonairechap

Sonny Seiler told me that even though Jim had a large collection of Nazi guns, knives, flags and paraphernalia stored in his home, they were never on display, nor was he interested in Nazi history. In 1979, a company filming an obscure made-for-TV Civil War movie created a nuisance in Monterey Square and virtually shut down Jim's antiques business. The filmmakers had covered two streets and the streets around Monterey Square with yellow mud to simulate a city square in the 1850s. The longer the film company stayed, the angrier Jim became.

Without thinking about the controversy he would ignite, Jim draped a large Nazi flag off a Mercer House balcony so the cameras wouldn't film his house. Later, when someone reminded Jim that a Jewish temple was across the square, he apologized for any offense. The mistake came back to haunt him repeatedly.

Jim developed a unique position within Savannah's social structure. Even though he was a rebel, respect and admiration for him continued to grow. Most of the people I interviewed liked Jim very much and agreed that he was very hard-working, not just as a deal-maker and expert, but as a man who actually restored antiques himself. His hands were calloused from working on the furniture he restored. No one doubted his high intelligence and pragmatism. A number of people said he was the most interesting person they had ever met. He had a great sense of humor, was a terrific host, and made his friends feel comfortable whenever they were in his presence. Jim was frequently described as charismatic and very much the southern gentleman. Though he was criticized for being gay, Jim was very conservative in his thinking in other ways—a southern chauvinist, according to one individual. Several people noted his genuine interest in people and a willingness to help people he liked. One friend said that if you shared a subject in which he was interested, he'd pick your brain. He'd learn from you.

Jim donated a number of valuable antiques to the Telfair Museum and cash to the Humane Society.

To be sure, there were downsides to his personality as well. The most common negative comment was that he was controlling and manipulative, a complaint frequently leveled at very successful people. There were also some significant issues with his business ethics, which I will address in the next chapter.

Carol Freeman was one of Jim's good friends. "He had a tremendous sense of humor, very dry wit, and he was very smart," she told me enthusiastically. "He always had such a positive attitude and he had such a tremendous sense of humor. He kept me in stitches."

Jim was known for his parties and, after meeting Jim, Carol went to all of them. "His parties were fabulous," she reminisced. "He was the consummate host. He really knew how to entertain. And he was so handsome, always looking so elegant."

In 1972 or 1973, Jim first showed up on her radar. She had gone to Mercer House to see a sideboard that Jim had. They got to know each other that day, sitting there on the veranda.

Mercer House party
Photo by Jeanne Papy

Carol looked at herself in those days as a kind of rebel, much as Jim was. She was not born into Savannah society, but her husband was. For a while, she rebelled, but then, she said, she straightened up: She learned to play golf, participated in the children's theater, the golf club, and most of the other activities in which Savannah society wives in that era were expected to participate.

Carol laughed as she told me about Jim's box of 5×7 file cards. Jim had personal handwritten notes on file cards for all the people who had ever been to his parties. He used them as the basis to decide who would be invited to his next party and who wouldn't. The kind of thing that would keep you off the invitation list was having a party and not inviting Jim. According to Carol, Jim knew everything going on socially in Savannah. Jim took great pleasure in deciding who he would favor and who he would "punish," but it was all in fun, and not at all malicious. He was mischievous.

On the first day of his trial, he suggested to Carol that they go to the staid, exclusive Oglethorpe Club for lunch. Bachelor sons of Gordon, Georgia, barbers were not members of the Oglethorpe Club, but Carol and her husband were. It was just like Jim to poke at Savannah society mores.

"Savannah was bizarre in a quiet, genteel way," Carol told me. "Some things were simply not discussed. People covered each others' asses. Homosexuality was not accepted and not discussed. Old Savannah society hasn't changed much. They don't care about money so much, just old families."

One of the best times Carol had with Jim was when they went in Jim's Jaguar to the polo matches at Rose Hill Plantation in Bluffton, South Carolina. He told Carol just what to wear. They were role-playing, after all. "We took a beautiful tablecloth, fine crystal, and the Czar's silver," Carol said. "If you have it, flaunt it," Jim told her.

As Carol talked about how much fun she had with Jim, it was clear that she dearly missed him: "He was kind, genteel, thoughtful, thoroughly enjoyable and a great friend."

Hairdresser Joel Moore gave me insight into Jim's wild streak. Joel had been rehearsing the opening of his new salon that was adjacent to the Peachtree Spa. For the opening, Joel had persuaded the spa to open its pool for the festivities, but the spa said only women. Jim stopped in at the rehearsal with his friend Iris Mock, but for some mischievous reason, he decided to strip off his clothes and swim naked in the pool.

One man that I interviewed was David Sands, a talented designer and decorator, who knew Jim professionally. Sands had wealthy clients who would buy Jim's antiques. During the interview, I mentioned that I toured Mercer House and noted that so many items in Jim's favorite downstairs room were prints, statues, and other artistic renderings of predatory birds and animals. Did this artistic collection provide some insight into Jim's character? Not so, Sands told me. Jim was a naturalist and loved paintings, prints, and statues of animals, including a framed wasps' nest and a turtle shell. Jim was never a hunter of animals, though—only a fisherman, he explained.

Chapter 9

Shady Dealings

When I first start interviewing Jim's friends and associates years ago, it never occurred to me that he might be involved in unscrupulous dealings. A number of his friends volunteered that Jim came across as trustworthy and credible. "His word was his bond," his friend Miriam K. Center told me. Then, when I interviewed the late Mike Hawk, who managed the Catherine Ward House Inn in Savannah's Victorian District, I heard something very specific about unethical and illegal activities going on with Jim's antiques restoration business. The more people I interviewed, the more they brought up frauds that Jim had perpetrated.

Mike Hawk was good friends with Douglas Seyle, who worked for Jim in his restoration shop for a number of years. Doug spoke at great length to Mike about some of the restoration activities that Jim had initiated. The workshop had some exceptionally talented craftsmen, like Barry Thomas, who could create excellent reproductions of antique furniture. Unfortunately, Jim employed the skills of these craftsmen to defraud some of his clients. These clients were typically clueless about the value of the antiques in their homes and were very impressed with Jim's expertise when it came to antiques. Here is how the fraud evolved with a hypothetical client.

"Amanda, this table is a disgrace," Jim told the wealthy matron who had a home full of valuable antique furniture that had been in her family for generations. "Look how scratched the top is and how stained the marble inlays are. I just hate to see this wonderful table in such poor shape. My boys could have this fine table restored to its original beauty in no time."

Amanda had never paid much attention to the old table and was embarrassed to hear Jim criticize its condition, so she let Jim restore it. When the table reached Jim's workshop, it was restored with great care and a perfect reproduction was made. The original antique table was shipped to another city and possibly overseas for sale, and the attractive reproduction was given to Amanda. Amanda was pleased with the table that looked exactly like the original, minus the scratches and stains. The risk to Jim was low. Amanda was selected for this fraud because she knew nothing about antiques and had enough money that she would not in her lifetime need to sell her antiques to make ends meet. The fraud may never have been discovered. Her heirs, if they paid any attention whatsoever, probably assumed that the handsome table was not one of her antiques.

Independently, I happened to interview another friend of Jim's who told me he had offered a trip to Europe in exchange for bringing through customs an expensive painting for him. The friend knew the arrangement was not on the up-and-up and refused to take him up on his offer.

Joe and Nancy Goodman (recent photo)

I interviewed Joe Goodman, the man closest to Jim. Joe's wife, Nancy, also knew Jim well. While they knew each other for decades, Joe worked for Jim for eight or nine years doing odd jobs. Jim was best man at Joe's first wedding. Jim trusted Joe completely and told him all the places where he hid large sums of cash in Mercer House. Jim was like a father to Joe, and Joe never forgot it.

In the midst of my long talk with Joe Goodman and his wife, he said, unprompted, "You know, Williams was involved in a few shady deals." Back in the 1968-69 timeframe, Joe and Jim took Jim's old pickup truck and drove up U.S. Route 321 to a big old house around Garnett in Hampton County, South Carolina, where Jim had visited a couple times before to impress the owners and win their trust.

The house belonged to two sweet old wealthy spinsters who offered them milk and cocoa. Jim laid on the charm very heavily. "Made them feel like queen bees," Joe recalled.

Evidently, on an earlier trip, Jim had set up the kind of fraud that was later perpetrated on "Amanda." The old ladies had an enormous antique mahogany table and 14 valuable Chippendale chairs with round-ball claw feet, made for some English duke. The chairs were badly scratched up and the finish darkened and damaged. Jim had offered to buy the chairs, but the ladies had refused, so he offered to restore them because Jim told them "he hated to see them in such bad shape."

Joe and Jim loaded the chairs into the pickup truck and drove back to Savannah, where Jim was going to have them crated and sent to a cabinetmaker in Philadelphia to have them reproduced. The unsuspecting old ladies would get back 14 chairs that were actually replicas of their original Chippendales, which Jim would then sell. When the 28 Chippendale chairs were returned from the Philadelphia craftsman, I was told by an eyewitness that only an expert could tell the originals from the replicas.

Jim engaged in this kind of trickery over a long period of time, The "Amanda" type incidents, according to Mike Hawk, occurred throughout the 1970s and 1980s. It is not clear how much, if anything, Jim's craftsmen, knew about the fraud. It's entirely possible that the only employee in the shop that knew was Doug Seyle, who was not one of the restorers. Most of Jim's former restorers have died and the only one that I was able to locate refused to speak with me.

One night, when Joe Goodman was at Mercer House with Jim, a stranger came to the back door very late with a Tiffany lamp. After examining the lamp, Jim paid him $15,000 cash at the door. The man left without a bill of sale. Jim explained to Joe that frequent back-door transactions like that were one of the reasons he kept so much cash in the house. One can surmise that the Tiffany lamp was probably stolen, although some cash-strapped Savannah "blueblood" may have sold the family heirlooms this way to avoid embarrassment.

Tombee plantation house

In the mid-1970s, Jim restored two homes in Beaufort County, South Carolina. One was Barnwell House and the other was Tombee, a plantation house on St. Helena's Island, nicknamed after its original owner, Thomas B. Chaplin. The restoration of Barnwell House was much more costly than Jim had anticipated. The fall of 1975 was particularly difficult as he struggled to complete the work so he could put the house on the market the following spring.

Mercer House was burglarized twice in 1975. Jim was at Tombee when the first burglary occurred. His entire collection of jade and silver was stolen. Over time, Savannah police were able to recover some of the items. In December, while Jim slept upstairs, a thief stole 13 guns, mostly antiques, and 650 rounds of ammunition, according to the police report.

"The burglar stole only weapons," Jim said, "and he obviously knew where they were because the only drawers that were open in the house were where the weapons were and I always thought it was an inside job, which made me very nervous."

Fortunately for Jim, the stolen property was insured, and he was able to use the insurance money to cover some of the Barnwell House restoration costs. Unfortunately, he sold Barnwell House at a loss in 1976.

A fascinating story came up repeatedly, although there is no way to confirm it. One of Jim's friends, Albert "Bert" Adams, was an art teacher with a master's degree at who taught at Savannah's Country Day School. Bert, who was tall and stocky, was nicknamed "The Viking." Allegedly, Jim had Bert stage the first burglary of the silver and jade pieces, and possibly the second burglary of guns and ammunition as well. Bert was to find places faraway from Savannah to sell the silver. It was important that the distinct silver and jade pieces did not show up in antique shops in the Savannah area. If they did, the insurance fraud could be traced back to Bert and Jim. However, the plan supposedly hit some snags, and some of the silver and jade eventually showed up in the Savannah area, which is how Savannah police recovered them. This snag created a liability for Jim and Bert. Bert Adams died of carbon monoxide poisoning in 1979.

Among the insiders who shared the silver theft story, Bert's death caused alarm. They could not understand how Bert, who worked on cars and motorcycles all his life, would have had his garage door down on a hot, humid mid-September day while he was working on his car with the engine running. No autopsy was performed, and Bert was buried the next day.

Chapter 10

Racing Down a Dead-End Street

For most of his short life, Danny Hansford seemed doomed to end up in prison, a mental institution, or a cemetery. His fits of rage, expressed in unprovoked violence, may have been ingrained and intensified by a very unstable home life.

Danny Lewis Hansford was born on March 1, 1960, the youngest of Charles and Emily Hansford's three sons. Danny's mother divorced his father in 1962 and married Edward Bannister that same year. When Danny was a boy, his father moved to South Carolina to marry again. In 1969, his father took his gun and committed suicide. Danny's mother, Emily, had one daughter with Edward Bannister. She then divorced him in 1970 and married Donald Olsen. The next year, she divorced Olsen as well. Afterwards, she suffered a nervous breakdown and was treated by Dr. Abraham H. Center in Savannah. All of these events added up to a difficult and unsettling life for Emily and her children. Danny always told people he looked like his father, and that was why Emily hated him and "throwed" him away.

All three Hansford boys—Johnny, Billy, and Danny—had, at some point in their adolescence, lived at the Bethesda Home for Boys. Danny was there for most of 1972. The Bethesda Home was founded in 1740 as an orphanage on 500 acres of farmland south of the city of Savannah by evangelist George Whitefield. By the 1970s, Bethesda was no longer just for orphans, it also took boys from struggling single-parent homes, like Emily's family. At that time, the boys normally lived on campus and attended local schools, and some went home for the weekends. Today, the home has been transformed into Bethesda Academy, a private residential and day school for boys in grades 6 through 12.

It's hard to say how Danny fared at Bethesda, as the records from that era no longer exist. By age 13, Danny had come to the attention of school authorities because he failed most of his classes and skipped school excessively. The principal held Danny back in 1973, after he missed 45 days of school. In 1974, he missed 63 days of school, and school officials held him back once more in 1975. His grades were mostly Fs and Ds, but he did receive an A in art class. With less than an eighth-grade education and no interest in learning a trade, his job prospects were very poor. Instead, he picked up his education on the streets of Savannah, experimenting with LSD, marijuana, cocaine, various uppers and downers, and selling his sexual favors for money to buy drugs and alcohol.

By 1975, Emily realized that she could not cope with her son. The situation at home became progressively worse. On August 4, she asked the Chatham County Juvenile Court to take him because he was beyond her control. Danny refused to obey her, used drugs and alcohol, associated with friends of questionable character, and even struck her on July 2.

His case worker recommended Gould Cottage, a home for poor children. On August 20, Danny was ordered to live there. But Danny couldn't deal with the Gould Cottage rules and returned home, where he stayed for a few days and then disappeared without his mother's permission.

On August 27, Danny stole a pistol from his mother's bedroom. She filed a new petition in juvenile court, stating again that he was beyond her control. A month later, police arrested him and placed him in the county's juvenile detention center.

On October 10, he was put on probation and released to his mother, but he was back in court 14 days later for beating up his younger sister, Tracy Bannister. He hit her in the face and gave her a black eye. Judge Dickey placed Danny in the county's community treatment center, hoping that he would straighten up if he received therapy for his emotional problems. This option did not work out well for his mother because she had to provide transportation to and from the center, and it interfered with her employment.

In early December 1975, Danny tore a door off its hinges in the family's home when his mother refused to let him go to a friend's house. Emily took him to the Memorial Hospital Emergency Room to bandage up his hands and to have him evaluated for personality problems. After listening to Emily's story, Dr. Lester Haddad ordered a mental status exam. The test showed that Danny was alert and not hallucinating, but his violent rages were not normal. The doctor told Emily that her son needed further assessment by a psychiatrist and persuaded her to send him to Georgia Regional Hospital, a public hospital for the mentally ill. Dr. Haddad gave Danny a preliminary diagnosis of a personality disorder.

A psychiatrist at Georgia Regional, Dr. Simon Spiriosa, diagnosed 15-year-old Danny as having "unsocialized aggressive behavior" with emotional instability. Dr. Spiriosa wanted to keep Danny at the hospital for treatment, but Danny did not want to stay, and Emily did not agree to his continued hospitalization.

Every few months during 1976 and the first part of 1977, Danny's case worker or his mother petitioned the court about him: when given a choice of going to school or gainful employment, he would do neither. Instead, he ran away from home, refused to obey his mother; took a large knife to school, and violated his probation. Police arrested Danny several times and Judge Dickey confined him to the Chatham County Juvenile Detention Center for short periods of time.

In October 1976, Mrs. Penny Mitchell complained to the court that Danny threw a screwdriver and hit her son in the leg. Danny said he did it because Mitchell's son called him a "fag." Mitchell could have prosecuted Danny, but decided not to press charges if the court would convince Danny to leave her son alone.

In March 1977, Judge Dickey decided that it would be in the best interest of Danny and society to confine him in the Chatham County Jail [separate from adult offenders] until he could be transferred to a state reform school in Augusta. It's unlikely that he was ever sent to Augusta; because his mother was back in court again August 26 seeking to restrain him from causing bodily harm to her family and herself. Danny was living on West Jones Street in Savannah when police arrested him on October 10 for criminal conspiracy to burglarize Solomon's Drug Store on Bull Street.

On Dec. 16, 1977, Danny joined the US Air Force Reserves at the age of 17. It's very possible that after the October arrest, a judge persuaded Danny to enlist in the military rather than face prison or detention in Augusta. He was stationed at the Charleston, SC, airbase. Once he finished basic training, he enrolled in a training program for aircraft maintenance, but never completed it.

Danny Hansford
Victim

Sources familiar with Danny's military service said that he lasted only five or six months before he was discharged for behavior that was not tolerated in the military. He continuously showed up late for training with a dirty, wrinkled uniform, started a fistfight with another reservist, exhibited a generally poor attitude about the Air Force, and expressed a clear desire to leave the service. The counselors who tried to help him believed that he needed psychiatric help and was not suited to an Air Force career.

Once he returned to Savannah in the summer of 1978, it didn't take long for Danny to create problems for his mother. In early July, Emily signed a complaint against him for stealing a tire and the battery from of her car.

On June 30, 1979, Danny rented an apartment at The Confederate Manor. He had been drinking heavily and was angry about the noise that another tenant was making. He flew into a rage at his landlord, Howard Loper, who told Danny that he was doing everything he could to keep peace in the building. Not liking his landlord's answer, Danny picked up a chair and threw it through Loper's window. After that, Danny beat him up, damaged his car with a brick, and knocked down a post lamp. Loper, in fear of his life, picked up a wooden banister and beat Danny's head and arms. After the police arrested Danny, who was lacerated and bloody, they took him to the Memorial Hospital emergency room for stitches. After that, because emergency room physicians considered Danny a psychiatric emergency, the police took him to Georgia Regional Hospital, where he had been sent in 1975 after attacking his sister.

Nina A. Kelly, an experienced nurse at Georgia Regional Hospital, performed a preliminary assessment of Danny when he arrived on June 30. She evaluated him as homicidal and acutely psychotic. He was very angry and did not want to be admitted into the psychiatric hospital.

Dr. Aurel Teodorescu of Georgia Regional described him as hostile, aggressive, and psychotic. He said that Danny had lost contact with reality. The doctor ordered him to be secluded. The orderlies had to tie him down with leather straps to a steel cot to keep him from injuring the staff and other patients. Danny needed professional treatment, but he refused to get it. The next day, he asked to be signed out against medical advice. Danny said he did not understand why he was sent to Georgia Regional and wanted to get out as soon as he could.

Sometime in late spring or early summer, Danny rode up to Mercer House on a bike and stopped Jim Williams as he was getting out of his car with his psychologist friend, Dr. Lance Hamburger. Danny was looking for work. Jim hired him as a part-time employee to strip the finishes and upholstery from furniture and to help clean and repair two huge crystal chandeliers that had been damaged in transit from New York to Savannah. Danny worked part-time on and off throughout 1979.

One of Danny's most interesting relationships was with his very attractive girlfriend, Debbie. Because Debbie knew Danny so intimately over a period of time, investigators for both the prosecutor and the defense eagerly interviewed her about their relationship and Danny's personality.

Debbie was working behind the bar at O'Reagin's Lounge on Ogeechee Road when she met Danny around the beginning of February 1980. At the time, she was living in a trailer on Countryside Drive with another young woman who was dating Danny's best friend, George Hill.

In a lengthy interview with J.D. Smith, one of the prosecutor's investigators, Debbie said she dated Danny a week or so after she met him and went out with him until his death more than a year later. "It wasn't a super, super steady thing. I wasn't going out with any other guys, but still," she said. "Well, Danny was a really unstable person. He could be in a good mood one second, and then he could get real mad real easy." When Smith asked whether the sharp mood swings were his normal personality or became apparent only when he drank, she said, "Danny and his friend

George drank all the time and Danny had a temper when he drank."

"He was fun at first," she told another investigator. "And he took me out to dinner at several places... And we'd go out dancing and things like that. When Danny wasn't stoned, he'd open car doors for you. He was sweet. He had like two different personalities. The real weird one and then he'd be sweet."

At the trailer that she and her girlfriend shared, Danny went out of his way to be cruel to her roommate. "He busted up her mirror that she had just bought and tore up her high school senior pictures," Debbie recalled. "And then he just stood there and laughed about it. You know, uncalled-for violence. And [her girlfriend] was crying. He got his kicks out of doing stuff like that. He told [her] she was ugly and fat and then he'd laugh. It was so much fun to him. He had a strange thing about hurting people's feelings. I'd tell him, 'Wait a minute. You can't go on doing this stuff to people.'"

Danny took Debbie to Mercer House many times during 1980 and 1981. Sometimes George Hill went along, too. Usually, they entertained themselves by playing cards, Atari games, or Psycho Dice—a game that Jim invented—and drinking.

Debbie said when they were together, nothing in Danny's behavior even hinted that he had any homosexual tendencies. Nor did Jim's behavior around her and Danny suggest that there was any sexual relationship between the two men. Danny was just too possessive for her to think that he wasn't strictly heterosexual. Debbie said that Danny didn't come on to her sexually very often except when they were at Mercer House.

Both Jim and Danny had deceived her about the reason why Danny was living at Jim's house. "The way both of them put it on to me was that Danny was one of Jim's charity cases, but that he was a super-good worker so he gave him a place to stay because Danny, him and his mother didn't get along at all."

Despite his growing obsession with Debbie, he didn't always treat her well. "Danny did a lot of drugs. He'd get mean," she said. "One time I told him to take me home, because he was too stoned and acting kind of crazy, and he slapped me in the face, and pushed me out of the car downtown. And I was walking home. Then he drove around the corner, it was on one of the squares, and he drove around and came back and wanted me to get in the car. And I didn't want to get back in the car with him. Finally he talked me into letting him take me home. But he did not take me home. He drove by Abercorn Street and I don't know where and he got pulled over for speeding. But anyhow, the police had to take me home that night."

According to Frank "Sonny" Seiler, Jim's attorney, Debbie recalled another instance when she and Danny were driving back from Tybee Island, a popular seaside vacation spot outside the metropolitan Savannah. Suddenly, he got mad at her, beat her up, and made her get out of the car. On a lonely road at night, he left her to find her own way home—alone.

Danny just couldn't stay out of trouble. On June 18, 1980, he attacked Robert Croyle, a landscape maintenance contractor. Croyle had been spraying 14 apartments for roaches for one of his clients, landlord Alvin Neeley, and knocked on the door of Danny's apartment. Neeley had given Croyle passkeys to each apartment and permission to enter the apartments and spray them if the tenant wasn't at home.

"I would start at the bottom," Croyle said, "and work up to the top floor. So Hansford's was the last apartment I got to: he lived on the top.

"And I knocked on the door. There was no answer. I knocked again and waited. No answer, so I used the passkey. I couldn't get in the door because the chain was on inside and thought, well, he has to be here, so I hollered, 'Danny, it's Bob, spraying for roaches.'

"No response. So I called out again and there was no response. I locked the door back, sprayed the hallway, went home, had lunch, and went to sleep. About a couple hours later, there was a knock on my door (that) woke me up, and it was Danny Hansford.

"He yelled, 'You sprayed my cat with roach spray!' and he punched me in the eye and then turned around like he was walking off and I said, 'Wait a minute!' and he turned back around with a ring and hit me on the chin. It had a little thing sticking out to slice with. I had to have six stitches." (Danny had a piece of jewelry that he called his "fighting ring." On one side, it looked like a wedding band. On the other side, it had something that looked like a flattened nail with a triangular point at the end. He used to brag that he could tear a man's face to pieces with it.)

"And then he hit me in the knee and banged my head against the pavement," Croyle continued. "At this point, I grabbed ahold of him and got him on the ground and held him down. My hands are longer—arms are longer than his and he couldn't touch me. I said, 'Now, just stop it!'

"Finally, he quit flailing at me at arm's length. I told him, 'I'm going to let you up, but I'm going to go in the house and call the police and let them handle this,' which I did."

Well aware of Danny's reputation for violence, Croyle swore out a warrant. Danny asked Neeley to fire him, but instead Neeley told Danny to find somewhere else to live. Within a month, Danny had still not been served with the warrant because they weren't able to find him. However, Danny found Croyle and was ready to attack him again.

"I was coming back from the library down at City Hall with some books," Croyle said. "When I got up to Madison Square, Hansford was circling the square, hollering out his window, 'I'm going to get you! I'm going to get you!'

"He stopped his car and got out with the baseball bat and came after me. Of course, I didn't let him get close enough, hollering over to this lady that ran the restaurant over there, 'This fellow's attacking me with a baseball bat. Call the police.'

"She saw it and she yelled back, 'I'm going to do it right now.' And he heard that, and so he got back in his car and took off. I made a police report on that."

Shortly after he attacked Robert Croyle, Danny was hospitalized, but this time, the violence was inwardly directed. On August 7, 1980, Danny announced to Jim that he had taken 49 tablets of Jim's Limbitrol, a commonly prescribed combination of Librium, a mild tranquilizer, and Elavil, an antidepressant. Jim didn't believe him. When Danny passed out, Jim realized he wasn't faking, called his physician and, upon his advice, called an ambulance. By the time Danny reached the Memorial Hospital emergency room, he was unconscious—not in a deep coma, but unable to answer any questions or cooperate with any tests. Doctors at the emergency room pumped his stomach, admitted him to the intensive care unit, and kept him there for three days. Dr. Patrick Brooks, the internal medicine physician on call the night Danny was brought in, said that 49 tablets of Limbitrol can be a very lethal dose.

Danny's mother and Jim both told the doctor about Danny's violent, aggressive, and antisocial behavior. Jim said Danny had attempted suicide once before at Mercer House, although it was not documented in medical records at Memorial Hospital. His mother said he had homosexual tendencies, was a "charmer, who was often able to get his way," and had abused a number of different drugs. "As a child," Emily said, he was a breath-holder. He would turn blue and sometimes lose consciousness." The day after Danny was brought in, Brooks said, he became violent and verbally abusive in the ICU when he awoke, saying things that the doctor wouldn't dare to repeat. Brooks asked for a psychiatric evaluation, which is routine when a patient comes in with a drug overdose and a history of emotional problems. Danny was then transferred to Clark Pavilion, the secure psychiatric unit at Memorial Hospital.

After the suicide attempt, Danny left Savannah for several months, staying with his brother in Florida and working in a gas station. He had returned to Savannah and was living at 515 Lincoln Street when he was arrested for drunk driving on October 22. On October 30, Danny pleaded guilty to the two attacks on Robert Croyle. He listed Mercer House as his address. Jim's attorney, Robert Duffy, handled the matter.

Most of the people I interviewed who knew Danny had unfavorable views of him. Jim's close friends could not understand why such an attractive, intelligent, and cultured man like Jim would have anything to do with him. Not surprisingly, Jim did not introduce Danny to the socialites and luminaries that came to the famous Christmas parties nor to his wealthy clients. Still, a number of Jim's friends met Danny and they assessed his appearance and personality in considerably different ways.

As an adult, Danny was 5 feet, 10 inches tall, weighed about 155 pounds, had blue eyes, straight brown hair, and a brown mustache. He had tattoos on both arms: a Confederate flag and a marijuana leaf on the right arm, and a winged dragon-like figure and star-like figure on the left arm.

Joe Goodman, Jim's longtime friend, didn't think he was good-looking at all. Another man who worked for Jim said Danny was a "squirmy punk who would shrink away from people." A man who lived in Danny's neighborhood described him as "thin, not muscular, not bad-looking, but certainly not handsome." He added that Danny and his brothers were the neighborhood bullies. A salon owner who knew Danny called him "an unfixable car and a scumbag hottie. A wild child blessed with a large penis." Mike Hawk, who managed the Catherine Ward House Inn, had seen Danny several times in bars and disliked him intensely. To Mike Hawk, Danny came across as an untrustworthy, dangerous redneck, who was in no way physically attractive.

Some of the women I interviewed saw him somewhat differently. Jim's friend Diane Silver Berryhill told me that even though Danny "wasn't pretty, he had sex appeal. I could see why men and women were attracted to him." Ali Fennell, a bartender, likened Danny to a "rough diamond: attractive to look at, but rough around the edges. He was very good-looking, young and full of life."

Everyone seemed to agree that Danny was either high on marijuana or drunk most of the time. Nobody I interviewed thought Danny was nearly as attractive as Jude Law, who played him in the Clint Eastwood movie.

Jude Law during filming
Photo by Jeanne Papy

After Joe came into contact with Danny a few times, he asked, "Williams, what the hell are you doing letting this piece of shit live here? This kid is trouble and he's going to make you sorry someday."

As time went on and more of Jim's close friends came into contact with Danny, Jim manufactured a rationale for having this rude street hustler in his life. Jim told people that Danny was artistic and that he was trying to help him develop something positive in his life. Many were skeptical. Joe could not comprehend the relationship. Danny had repeatedly exploited and embarrassed Jim. Many of Jim's friends were aware of Danny's reputation as a male prostitute.

Finally, Joe asked, "Williams, why are you keeping this guy around?"

Jim answered simply, "He's good in bed."

There had to be more to it. Jim had access to many gay men. Perhaps something about Danny satisfied some inner, possibly unconscious, need. There may have been another more practical reason for Jim for putting up with Danny's continual demands for money, clothes, and drugs. Danny seemed to have the upper hand in private conversations with Jim, which Debbie had witnessed. Danny, who started his part-time employment in Jim's workshop, may have been aware that some of Jim's clients were being given perfect replicas of the antiques that they believed were being restored. Danny may have threatened to expose him.

Some of Jim's friends have shared their insight into the relationship with me. Miriam K. Center, a writer who knew both Jim and Danny, felt sorry for Danny. She saw him as a wild, crazy youngster who had been allowed to enjoy Jim's wealth, but not as an equal. Jim, she said, ate at good restaurants like the Chatham Club, but gave Danny money to eat at McDonald's.

Ali Fennell told me that Jim seemed to be attracted to danger and living on the edge. Danny was always high on weed and acted very cocky, she said. From what she could see, Danny played dumb, but was very street-smart. She couldn't really get to know him because he was always too drugged. She rarely saw Jim and Danny together in public, except occasionally, when they met up at the end of the night.

Randy Shuman, a friend of Jim's, saw the relationship as Pygmalion-like. Jim tried to help Danny make something of himself. He dressed Danny and tried to refine his street manners. However, from what Randy could see, it was pure exploitation: Jim kept giving and Danny kept taking, and always wanting more. No matter what Jim gave Danny, he never had enough.

Danny closed out 1980 with another arrest on December 30 in Dania, Florida, for reckless driving, DUI, possession of marijuana, and driving with a suspended license. The license suspension was probably a result of the October arrest in Savannah for drunk driving.

Debbie, Danny's girlfriend, believed he had a death wish: "We'd drive by a cemetery and he would say, 'When I die I'm gonna have a headstone that's gigantic.' He'd always talk about death... I thought it was awfully strange for some his age to be talking about grave stones. He said Jim would pay for his gravestone. I don't know why he said that. I told him, 'You don't need to be talking about dying, as young as you are.'"

Chapter 11

Storm Clouds Gathering

The year 1981 began very badly for Danny Hansford. His violent behavior intensified, his girlfriend distanced herself, and his relationship with his benefactor was headed for the rocks.

In January, he launched another unprovoked attack. Barry Thomas was the talented restoration artist that managed Jim's basement workshop. At that time, Danny mostly worked on the main floor of Mercer House, doing things like stocking the bar, getting ice, and going to the post office. He only occasionally came down to the lower-level workshop. Barry very rarely ever talked to him or even saw him because Mercer House operated on two separate levels.

"There's Jim's private level upstairs, which is his own house," Barry explained, "and there's a shop downstairs, which is what I was more involved in. I tried to keep the separation between the two things very firm, so that Jim had a private dwelling to live in... I could run a business from it without causing a lot of inconvenience to him.

"I was leaving work one day about 5:30 when the incident occurred," Barry said. "During the day, I had observed Danny in the house, and he had been very moody the whole day, kind of sulking almost.

"And I was leaving with three other people, and I was coming up the staircase, and I heard steps coming down the staircase, and (at the same time) Jim came around the corner from the study into the main hall, which runs down the center of the house.

"And as I turned around to see where the footsteps were coming from, I saw Danny coming down the staircase and he was obviously very upset, because he just came at me and then went to kick me in the stomach, and his foot made contact with my stomach, but then Jim grabbed him and hauled him off with another fellow, and then Jim said to Danny, 'Get out of here!' I didn't know what was going on. I didn't know why he attacked me.

"I'd get on with Danny quite well. Whenever he came downstairs, we talked, and that's why I was so taken aback.

"A day or two later, when I came in, Danny was in the house. I walked up to him and I said, 'Danny, why did you attack me?' And he could not remember attacking me. He said, 'I don't remember I attacked you and I don't know why I attacked you.' And he wanted me to kick him and he said that would make him feel better.

"I told him what would make me feel better: if he would promise that he would not do that again. He promised, but the incident was left like that. I never found out why or for any reason.

"It scared the living hell out of me, and I was so taken aback, because I wasn't expecting it. Just the sheer fright of having someone attack you for no reason, it just makes you very nervous to be around someone when you don't know if this may happen again."

Subsequently, Danny's relationship with Jim began to fray, and Danny was less welcome as a permanent houseguest. A month after the attack on Barry Thomas, Douglas Seyle, one of Jim's employees, arranged for Danny to rent the carriage house on his mother's property at 101 East 36 Street, starting in February.

At the end of February, Danny was in trouble again. Danny and George Hill, his best drinking buddy, enjoyed picking fights. Earl LeFevre, a mechanic with Gulfstream, had lived on Key Street for 20 years. Both Danny and George Hill had lived in that same neighborhood. One day, Danny and George went to LeFevre's house to see his son. When his son left the house to talk to them,

Danny and George threatened him with bodily harm. LeFevre came out to protect his son, and George hit him, shouting, "I don't have to take any shit from you, either." LeFevre ended up fighting George, while his son fought with Danny. After Lefevre's wife said she was calling the police, Danny and George left, but not before George broke down LeFevre's front door, warning him that he hadn't heard the last of it. Lefevre went to court and filed complaints against Danny and George for threatening bodily harm, battery and destruction of property. George had to pay for damages.

Danny's relationship with Debbie was becoming increasingly strained. Danny constantly asked her to marry him. "It got old, you know," she said. "I told him, 'Please. Don't ask me to marry you. I'll go out with you tonight, but don't ask me to marry you.' I didn't want to get married to him, huh-uh. I didn't even move in with him."

When investigator J.D. Smith asked Debbie whether she thought that Danny was merely staying with Jim to hustle him, she answered, "Slightly, yeah." Debbie had no idea how Danny was paid for the work he did for Jim. She never saw him with a payroll check. She did notice that Danny was always borrowing money from Jim. The cash, she assumed, was an advance on Danny's pay.

Debbie said that Danny would get mad at Jim if he wouldn't lend him money. "He'd raise his temper and start really giving it to Jim. Danny cussed and stomped and hollered, screamed and threw a fit and told Jim he was going to hit him. He told me he would knock the shit out of Jim anytime. Didn't say he had [beaten Jim]. Talking big, trying to impress me. It was like a little temper tantrum or something, you know? Jim gave him the money. I heard that one time and I stepped back in the foyer and I was ready to go out the front door. I didn't want to stand there while they were arguing."

J.D. Smith asked Debbie if Danny had ever told her about Jim being involved in something illegal. Had Danny had ever mentioned to her that Jim had been involved with another antiques dealer on something shady that took place some time ago? There were a number of shady deals that Jim participated in, but this may have been related to the theft of silver from Mercer House that Jim had staged for insurance money. Might Danny have had something on Jim? Debbie said she didn't know about anything illegal at Mercer House, but Danny's behavior toward Jim caused her to have some doubts: "By the way that argument was that day when I was there, Danny acted like he was holding the upper hand—that he could get his way. And that was the way he acted around me, was that he could get his way, no matter what, around Jim Williams. He tried to act real powerful around me. That he could get all the money in the world, that Jim would give it to him."

Chapter 12

The Beginning of the End

In the early morning of April 3, 1981, the two men had a violent argument. According to Jim, Danny came by to borrow $20 to take Debbie on a date. Jim gave him the money, but Danny didn't leave. Instead, he got angry, saying that he'd spent the whole day working on his car with George Hill. Hill said he had no business with a car that he couldn't afford and that Danny should sell the car to George. Danny took it as an insult. Jim told Danny that George was his problem and not Jim's and walked away.

Apparently, that wasn't the response Danny wanted, so he smashed a new marble-top table, threw a bronze lamp against the wall, and smashed some Chinese porcelain and ivory figures. Then he took a cut-glass water pitcher and slammed it on the floor. The pitcher blew up like a grenade, and shards of glass stuck in Danny's arms. Jim said he thought Danny had calmed down and left the house. Jim locked the door and went upstairs to brush his teeth. Suddenly, he said, he saw Danny in the bathroom door with a crazy look on his face and one of Jim's German Luger pistols in his hand.

According to Jim, Danny asked, "How mad do I have to make you before you'll kill me?" and "Will this really shoot through the floor?" Then he shot a hole in the floor. When Jim tried to reason with him, he said Danny took the Luger and threw it from an upstairs window. Then he ran downstairs, grabbed another Luger that had been in the marble-top table he smashed, charged out into Monterey Square, and fired twice. Once Danny was out of the house, Jim called the police. Just as the police were coming into the square, Danny went back into the house, raced up the stairs, jumped into bed, pretended to sleep.

When the police got him up and asked him if he'd broken up the furniture downstairs, Danny told them it was none of their business. One of the cops saw the bleeding on Danny's arms caused by the shards of glass from the broken water pitcher and challenged him, asking him to explain how he got cut. Danny responded belligerently. Jim told the cops he wanted to press charges, so they arrested Danny.

The next day, Jim and Joe Goodman went to Judge Lionel Drew's Chatham County Recorder's Court. When Danny was brought up, Jim told the judge he was not going to press charges after all. He said that he thought that one night in jail would cure Danny a bit. Jim and Joe took Danny back to Mercer House, where they and Douglas Seyle started to clean up the mess from the night before.

Danny was feeling very low. He told Jim, "Man, I just don't know what happened. Sometimes I just go blank. I'm going to sell my car to pay for the damages. Then he laughed and said, "I sure outsmarted the fat cop last night, didn't I?"

"What do you mean?" Joe asked.

"They almost got me," Danny said, "but I got on that bed, and I convinced them I was asleep."

Debbie was dating Danny at the time, but she wasn't going out with him as much because he was "really starting to get on my nerves about this marriage thing all the time." She had a very different view of what caused the argument between Jim and Danny: Danny was jealous. On the night before the shooting, Debbie said that Danny was jealous because she had been at Mercer House drinking and playing dice with him and Jim. "He acted as if Jim was trying to put some moves on me, but he wasn't," she told an investigator. "Danny was super-jealous. God, I couldn't even look at or talk to anybody else when I was out with him and he got all mad about it.

"Danny acted as though he could really shoot a gun fantastic," Debbie said, although she had never seen him with a gun. Danny told her that he pulled and shot one of the 9 mm Lugers at the house that night. "Danny thought it was funny. But he'd get strange, boy... You could see a personality change in him. For no reason at all. Ooooh, yeah. He'd get some weird look in his eyes and get this crazy smile when he was... I dunno. He was sort of psychotic-looking."

For quite some time, Danny had been promising Debbie a gold chain necklace. She was so angry at what he had done to Jim on April 3 that she refused to see him for a week. He told her he was sorry. To make up for upsetting her, he was going to give her the necklace he had promised.

Danny didn't have the money to buy the gold chain necklace and he was desperate to shore up his deteriorating relationship with Debbie, so he pressured Jim to buy the necklace. Danny told Jim he wanted a gold chain necklace for himself, similar to one that he seen Jim wear.

Jim was quick to forgive Danny for the incident on April 3 and made reservations a week later, on April 10, to travel to London and Geneva with Danny on May 3. Jim suffered from hypoglycemia and was subject to fainting spells. Because Jim always took large sums of cash with him on his antiques-buying trips, he was concerned that he could be vulnerable to robbery.

Once Danny understood that on this trip, he would have to dress in a suit and tie all the time and leave his marijuana at home, he decided he didn't want to go. Joe Goodman, who was willing to take some time off work, would go instead.

Near the end of April, Jim bought the expensive (allegedly $400) necklace from a local jeweler and gave it to Danny, who then presented it to Debbie as something he had earned. Debbie told investigators that Danny deceived her and that much later she learned that Jim bought it for Danny.

On either April 29 or 30, Danny and Debbie were at Mercer House. Debbie was wearing the new piece of jewelry. At that time, Debbie believed that Danny had paid for the necklace and did not see any indication that Jim was upset to see her wearing it. About the same time, Debbie said that Danny asked her to commit him to a mental institution because he felt he was going off the deep end.

Chapter 13

Crisis—Jim's Story

The events that occurred between Jim and Danny at Mercer House on May 1, 1981, and the early-morning hours of May 2, were the focal point of four trials during the 1980s. Only Jim knew the truth about the crucial minutes early that Saturday morning when Danny Hansford breathed his last. This is Jim's story about the events of that fateful night.

Jim said that Danny came by Mercer House around 5:30 or 6 p.m., around the time the workshop staff left for the weekend.

One of Danny's complaints was that he didn't have any prospects for a real job. His intelligence or talents had been dulled by heavy use of alcohol and drugs. When he was given the opportunity to learn aircraft mechanics in the Air Force Reserves and antique restoration at the hands of the excellent craftsmen Jim had in his workshop, Danny couldn't stick with it. He became very frustrated and blamed everyone but himself.

Still, Jim was patient with him and offered to pay for training that could translate into a decent career. Jim had paid for several of his restorers to take specialized classes in skills that made them more valuable. Because Danny loved Atari computer games, Jim suggested that he ought to look into computer vocational school.

Danny seemed interested, so Jim called his friend Bruce Muncher, a computer programmer in Hinesville, Georgia, a little after 9:30 p.m. Bruce gave Jim information about cost and housing at a vocational tech school in northern Georgia.

Danny wanted to see a movie that night, so they went to the Weis drive-in around 10:30. Jim indulged Danny and sat through one the three zombie movies showing that night: "Dawn of the Dead," "Walk of the Dead," and "Curse of the Living Dead."

Jim Williams, May 1981
Copyright Savannah Morning News

Jim said that he believed that Danny had smoked eight or nine joints, consumed a half-pint of Wild Turkey bourbon, and had started on a second half-pint, but he was not drunk. They returned to Jim's house around 12:30 a.m.

They played backgammon and Atari in the living room for what Jim called "a real long time." Danny began to complain about his personal life, particularly three people—his mother, George Hill, and Debbie. The theme of the complaints was the one Danny most often voiced: "Everybody always throws me away." His mother hated him and had him put into institutions. George Hill wanted his '67 Camaro because Danny couldn't afford to maintain it on his part-time pay. Debbie got his "golden" necklace and then she humiliated him in a bar on River Street, and "made a fool out of him."

Jim claimed that Danny talked about these three people rapidly, in "a very high tone of voice. All of a sudden his personality snapped. It snapped just exactly like a Dr. Jekyll-Mr. Hyde situation. He turned into a raging madman, and he stood up and said, 'Those games. Those games have caused this whole thing.' Then he stomped right through the Atari set and the thing flew to pieces. Next, he took what was left of that half-pint of bourbon out of his back pocket and smashed it on the floor."

Jim said he told Danny to get out of his house immediately. Danny was still raging. Jim claimed that he had seen Danny like that before, but he'd always thought he could handle him. This time he couldn't. He left the living room to go to his study to call the police.

Danny had never physically threatened Jim before, but, Jim said, Danny grabbed him and shouted, "You are sick! Why don't you do everybody a favor and go out in the woods and die?" Then he threw Jim against an interior door with such force that he bounced back.

Jim said, "I kept talking to Danny but Danny wasn't talking in the same conversation with him. He was talking about a different world. It was as though I wasn't there. I just happened to be in his way." Then, Jim said he rushed into his study and picked up the phone just as Danny came in and screamed, "Who are you calling?"

Jim said that he had to think quickly. He was too afraid to try to call the police. Jim told him that he was calling Joe Goodman to tell him the trip to Europe was off. Earlier, Danny had complained that Jim had given Danny's trip away.

Jim said Danny sat down across the desk from him while he dialed Joe's number and told him the trip was off. Joe said that was all right with him. Then Danny snatched the phone out of Jim's hand and told Jim, "Don't lay that on me." Danny said, "Joe, I hope there's no hard feelings." Joe said later that he told Danny not to worry about it. Joe's girlfriend, Nancy Rushing, wondered at the time if Jim had been under duress when he made the call.

Jim said that Danny then picked up a silver tankard and said, "This silver tankard has just about made its mind up to go through that painting over there," meaning a large 18th-century painting.

Jim said he told Danny, "You're not going to tear my house up anymore. Now you get out!"

Danny answered, "Well, I'm leaving this town. Savannah's never been any good for me. I'm leaving this town tomorrow."

Jim tried to reason with him. "Danny, whatever you want to do. I thought you were going to go to school."

Danny repeated that he was leaving Savannah tomorrow and left the room. Jim said that he heard loud sounds coming from the hall. Danny returned to the study with a loaded German Luger in his hand and said, "I'm leaving this town tomorrow, but you're leaving tonight."

Jim said, "The minute I saw that loaded Luger, I reached in my drawer there, pulled it (the Luger in Jim's desk drawer) out, had the gun in my hand coming out. I was coming up from my seated position when a bullet was fired at me. I felt the breeze by my right arm. I'd never been as scared in my life, and I stood up and as fast as I could pull the trigger, I shot. That's exactly what happened." Jim said he fired more than once in rapid succession.

Jim said, "With the gun still in my hand, worn out in every capacity. I couldn't believe the whole thing. I walked over there and I just looked at the body and I thought, 'What on earth has happened? What caused this to happen?'

"I looked at him and I just—emotionally, it was hideous. I've just never done anything in my whole life before this and this just came on me all at once and it just came down like a storm, like a bolt of lightning striking, and suddenly I saw he was just—he was dead, very dead as far as I could see.

"I did not touch him. I don't think I touched him at all and I went to the telephone." He called his good friend Joe and said,

"Goodman, I just had to shoot Danny. Come down here as fast as you can." Jim didn't say that Danny was dead. Joe initially told Nancy that he was going alone, but Nancy was afraid of Danny and insisted that she go with him.

Next, Jim called his attorney, Robert Duffy, and then he called the police.

Joe and his girlfriend arrived at Mercer House at approximately 3 a.m., the same time as the police. Jim met Cpl. Anderson and several other officers at the door and told them that he shot his houseguest because the man had tried to kill him. Jim showed the police and Joe where Danny's body was lying in the study. An officer had Joe and his girlfriend stay in one of the other downstairs room. They told Jim to stay in the library in the back of the house while the police photographer and others examined the scene.

Initially Jim appeared calm and in control, but not long after the police arrived, the night's events caught up with him. He felt sick and slouched down in his chair. Nancy and one of the policemen helped lay him out on the sofa in the library. He passed out and one of the officers called for an ambulance. The paramedics gave Jim some oxygen and an EKG. Afterwards, he awakened.

Later that morning, police arrested Jim and took him to the Chatham County Jail. Jim called Joe once again and told him to bring $25,000 in cash from Mercer House to bail him out.

www.crimescape.com

Chapter 14

Gone but Not Forgotten

Debbie learned about Danny's death when her girlfriend showed her the morning paper. Later, George Hill told Debbie and her friend that Danny was a male prostitute and that he had a sexual relationship with Jim. Both women were shocked and disgusted.

Danny Lewis Hansford's grave

Jim was not going to miss the Fabergé sale and the opportunity to add to his cherished collection of jeweled Fabergé eggs, cigarette cases, snuff boxes, etc. The court allowed Jim to go as long as his bond was raised to $100,000. Once again, he asked Joe to go with him to safeguard his health and the large sums of cash he took along for his purchases. Three days after the shooting on May 6, Jim and Joe left on a plane to London, and then later to Geneva.

As the local media became fully engaged in reporting the shooting, Danny's troubled and tarnished reputation was exposed. While a number of Jim's friends knew or at least suspected he was gay, once the nature of his relationship with a violent and marijuana-dependent male prostitute was known, it became a scandal. The acceptance by Savannah's elite that Jim had worked for so diligently began to unravel.

On Friday, June 12, Chatham County Prosecutor Spencer Lawton presented his evidence to a grand jury, which indicted Jim for premeditated murder ("with malice aforethought," in legal terminology). The indictment was shocking and very damaging to the reputation of a respected antiques dealer with no history of violent behavior. Worse for Jim, Danny's mother, Emily Bannister, the woman who repeatedly rejected her son, immediately filed a $10 million-plus civil lawsuit against Jim for murdering her son— "execution-style."

Jim did not behave like a man who was guilty. He went to Europe a second time that year to buy antiques and, as usual, hosted his famous Christmas party for Savannah's socialites. Reportedly, some invited guests did not attend because they thought having the party the same year as the shooting was in bad taste.

www.crimescape.com

Chapter 15

The First Trial

George E. Oliver
(portrait)

Chatham Superior Court Judge George E. Oliver presided over the first three of Jim's four trials. He was appointed to the Chatham Superior Court judgeship in 1970 and kept that post until he reached mandatory retirement. After that, he took on the role of senior judge. He considered himself a politician of the best kind and a lifelong Democrat.

In a *Savannah Morning News* interview, his friend Frank Cheatham Jr. quipped, "Legend has it that when George was born, the first thing he did was to shake hands with the doctor and wink at the nurse. He's been shakin' and winkin' ever since."

Oliver was a Methodist Sunday school teacher and a leader in the local Masonic lodge. Like attorney Frank "Sonny" Seiler, Oliver was a big Georgia Bulldogs fan.

Leading the prosecution team was Chatham County's new
district attorney, Spencer Lawton Jr. He was a soft-spoken, serious
young man from a respected old Savannah family. Always a
victim's advocate, Lawton was known for his compassion for the
poor. He had unseated the Ryan family, which had enjoyed a 30-
year hold on the district attorney's office. Joe Ryan handed the
office down to his son Andrew "Busby" J. Ryan III," who had just
completed one term. Busby was expected to win another term
when Lawton jumped into the Democratic primary race. Lawton's
reputation as a man of principle earned him significant support
from the black community, which helped him win the subsequent
Democratic runoff and the race against the Republican candidate.

The other members of Lawton's team were Deppish Kirkland,
his chief assistant, and Robert Sparks, an assistant with the state's
Prosecuting Attorney's Council.

Spencer Lawton Jr. (recent photo)

Bobby Lee Cook, a well-known attorney from the small town of
Summerville, Georgia, in the northwest part of the state, was the

lead defense counsel. Former prosecutor Stan Irvin described Cook in 2009: "Bobby Lee Cook was an old-school trial attorney, regarded as one of the 'deans of criminal defense attorneys.' He is tall, lanky, has long gray hair, a goatee and mustache, gold rimmed glasses, and continues to wear classic three-piece suits when many no longer do. He arrives at court in a Rolls Royce, yet maintains the touch of a commoner. He is a southern gentleman: kind, polite and courteous... He was a legend in the South."

Whenever a super-lawyer is brought in from another city, a talented local defense attorney is usually added to the team. In this case, the local attorney was John Wright Jones, who at that time was best known for his defense in a case against Army Rangers accused of killing a gay businessman. Lawton lost that very controversial case, which was his first big case as the new DA.

Emily Bannister came to the trial with her second oldest son, Billy Hansford. Neither the prosecution nor the defense wanted her in the courtroom, so both sides subpoenaed her as a possible witness to keep her out. However, they could not keep her out of the court house, so she and her son sat patiently outside the courtroom in the hallway.

The jury was selected on January 25, 1982, and consisted of six men and six women.

The next day, Lawton told the jury that he would prove that Jim had murdered Danny in cold blood and with malice and forethought. Lawton believed that Jim had planned the murder a month earlier when he concocted a hoax in an April 3 incident to make Danny appear like to be a dangerous madman. After shooting Danny in May, Lawton was convinced that Jim had staged the crime scene to make it look like self-defense. When it was Bobby Lee Cook's turn to address the jury, he promised them he would prove that Danny was a violent man who had initiated the attack on Jim, who had no criminal record.

An Impassioned Prosecution

Lawton detailed the prosecution's rationale for its theory that the shooting was premeditated and the crime scene was contrived to make the shooting look like self-defense. These theories served as the basis for his statements to the court and his witnesses' testimony during the trial. At a later date, Lawton incorporated this information in his Williams case history and summary, a document published for his staff.

Lawton expressed his fervent belief that the relationship between Jim and Danny was "mutually exploitive, but not equally so: Hansford, in his naïve, coarse and reckless youth, no doubt thought he was taking advantage of Williams, who gave him money, clothes, car, jewelry and magnificent surroundings. But in the antique dealer he had met a pro, one who held all the cards. Williams was a sophisticated manipulator who could easily bestow money and trips to Europe; but he could just as easily withhold them. And Danny Hansfords could be had at a dime a dozen."

Thirty-six minutes to contrive the scene

To prove Jim had staged the scene of the shooting, Lawton had to demonstrate to the jury that Jim had enough time after he shot Danny to damage the antiques supposedly destroyed by Danny's rampage. He also had to show that Jim had time to make changes to the death scene so that it looked as if Danny had shot at him.

The amount of time that elapsed between the shooting and Jim's call to the police was critical to making the prosecution's case. There were two calls that morning between Jim and Joe Goodman—one to cancel the European trip, and one about the shooting. Danny's presence on the first phone call established a time at which Danny was still alive. The second call established a time when Danny had been shot. One witness would determine the times of those two calls.

Lawton began by establishing that Jim had called the police at 2:58 a.m. on May 2. The officers were close by and arrived at Mercer House within a couple of minutes around 3 a.m. That was a matter of record. Soon after the shooting, the police questioned Joe about the timing of the calls and Lawton used Joe's statement at that time to determine that there were approximately 36 minutes between the time Jim called Joe to tell him that he shot Danny and the time Jim called the police.

Joseph Goodman in Court
Copyright Savannah Morning News

Lawton's goal was to get Joe's testimony on the trial record as to the timing and the content of the two calls Jim made to him. Jim made the first call to Joe to say, "I've got bad news. The trip to Europe was cancelled."

Joe said, "Jim and I talked for a few seconds, or maybe a minute. I don't know. I was just awakened, you know, out of a dead sleep."

Then Joe said that Danny told him, "I hope there's no hard feelings," and Joe answered, "No, there's no hard feelings." Danny passed the phone back to Jim for a few seconds and Joe told him that he would see him sometime next week.

When Lawton asked him what he did after that conversation, Joe answered, "Well, I never turned the light on, so I just staggered back to my bed and smoked a cigarette. Nancy, my girlfriend, woke up, and she said, 'What's happened?' And I'd say shortly after our little conversation that must have lasted 10, 15, 20 minutes, I don't know—the phone rang again." When the phone rang a second time, it was Jim calling to tell Joe he had to shoot Danny.

Lawton needed to hear Joe repeat on the stand what he had said in his statement about how much time elapsed between the two calls. To Lawton's consternation, Joe answered, "I'd say between 15 and 30 minutes." Because Joe did not wear a watch, Lawton asked if he had looked at a clock. Joe explained the difficulty in doing so: "Well, my microwave clock sits kinda sideways from my couch and I had one phone in the apartment. It's a small apartment and you have to get out of your bed, walk around into a door and right at the door sits a table, a couch, and then kinda opposite, my microwave. It's an Amana with red lights, digital lights... but unless you're right up on it, the two's look like eight's sometimes, the four's look like five's sometimes, you've got to be dead up on it.

"I looked at the clock, but truthfully I can't really say it was exactly 2:25 or 2:30. I can just say a few minutes—not a few minutes—I'd say 15, 20, 30 minutes later, because me and Nancy, we laid in the bed and we talked and we kinda laughed a little bit and we couldn't go right back to sleep, but the lights were never on until after the second phone call."

This answer was not the one the prosecutor wanted. Joe's statement back in early May 1981 was inconsistent with what he was saying in court. Lawton wanted to show Joe a copy of his statement to refresh his memory, but Cook objected on the grounds that Lawton was leading the witness because Joe had not requested a copy of his statement.

Lawton then asked Joe what was said in the second conversation. Joe answered, "Come downtown quick. I just had to shoot Danny." Jim had not said that Danny was dead. Joe told his girlfriend that he was going to Jim's by himself. Nancy replied, "No. I'm going with you." Nancy was well aware of Danny's violent behavior and didn't want Joe to go to Mercer House alone. They hurriedly put on jeans and T-shirts and drove as quickly as they could to Jim's house, arriving at the same time as the police.

After some discussion, the judge permitted Lawton to ask Joe if he signed a statement in May of 1981 saying that the second call from Jim was around 2:20 to 2:25 a.m. Joe answered, "That's what I signed, yes."

Lawton wanted to know, "Are you now saying that that's untrue, or are you now saying that you can't remember or don't know?"

Joe said, "I can't be sure. In other words, it might be five or ten minutes one way or the other."

Lawton picked a time in between 2:20 and 2:25 in Joe's signed statement as the time of the second call—2:22 a.m.—to calculate the 36 minutes from the 2:58 a.m. call Jim made to the police in which Jim allegedly staged the crime scene.

After that, defense attorney John Wright Jones cross-examined Joe. He asked about the time it took them to get from his apartment to Jim's house. Joe said it probably took between seven and 10 minutes, driving down Drayton Street at 40 to 45 miles an hour. At that time there were no cars on the road.

Jones also asked him how Danny sounded when he spoke to him. Joe answered, "He—slurred words a little bit. I could tell he'd been drinking—but he sounded like Danny."

Then Jones asked why his girlfriend didn't want Joe to go by himself. Joe said, "She was scared of..." Lawton interrupted with an objection on the grounds that Joe was about to testify about a prior act of violence on Danny's part. The judge eventually agreed with Lawton. What Jones was permitted to ask Joe was if he was familiar with Danny's reputation: Joe answered that Danny's reputation was bad.

Lawton: The Crime Scene Was Staged (source: Lawton's case summary)

The position of the body:

"A person coming into the room would approach from behind and to the right of anyone sitting at the desk. As seen from behind the desk, Hansford's body lay face down in front of the desk, feet-to-left and head-to-right, the head being on the same right-front spot that Williams said Hansford was standing on when firing at him.

Courtroom model of death scene
Copyright Savannah Morning News

"He was in the classic, comic-book position of the dead gunman," Lawton explained. "(He was) chest-down on the floor, head face-down on the right cheek; left forearm under left shoulder like a child sleeping; right arm out at the shoulder level and bent, with the hand resting in the shooting position on the grip of the Luger pistol at about head level, right leg extended straight out, the left leg bent with the ankle lying across the right leg just above that ankle. He had obvious bullet wounds in his back and the back of his head (the shot to the chest didn't exit the body but lodged near the spine). Under his head and chest was a large pool of blood.

"On the back of the right hand (the one on top of the pistol grip) was a heavy deposit of blood, which had evidently been smeared—and a lighter area in the blood around the wrist, where some of it had apparently been rubbed off. There was no wound on the right hand, and no blood around it—or on the gun beneath it." Dr. Larry Howard, head of the state crime lab, testified that "it appeared from the police photos that the victim's right hand had been had been moved from underneath the body to extend above his head."

Lawton described what he believed was the clearest evidence of tampering with the death scene: "Over Hansford's legs (and facing his head) was an upright chair, upholstered and of heavy antique wood construction. One rear leg of this chair was firmly on top of the material of Hansford's right trouser leg.

Items on Jim's desk had been moved:

"On the desk, at the left-front and directly next to the right arm of the chair just mentioned, was an extinguished marijuana cigarette and a burn hole. The cigarette appeared to have been ground out on the leather desk top. A plastic bag of marijuana lay adjacent.

"Also on the desk, at the right arm of one seated there, was a stack of papers which had clearly been hit with a bullet, with papers and fragments strewn about the desk top, and on the floor behind and to the right of one seated there. And behind the desk, on the floor, was a damaged metal commemorative belt buckle in a leather pouch, which had evidently been in the stack of papers when it was hit.

"On top of the stack was an undamaged *TV Guide*, which had obviously been put there after the stack itself had been shot. Finally—also on top of the desk, directly in front of the seat—was a German Luger pistol. And on top of the pistol, including the grip, were paper fragments, indicating that the gun had been placed there before the adjacent pile of papers was hit.... In the seat of the desk chair were found lead fragments, presumed to be from the bullet which had struck the pile of papers and the belt buckle—and indicating that no one was sitting in or obstructing the seat when the bullet was fired into the pile."

The shooting and subsequent staging of the scene:

"Accepting that at some point they were together in the study and arguing, as Williams claimed, and that the canceled trip was a point of contention, it's plausible to imagine that Hansford, sitting in the chair across from Williams and to his left, in spiteful anger, snubbed out a marijuana cigarette on the leather desk top. Whereupon, Williams reached into a drawer at his right hand, pulled out a Luger and shot Hansford. As he saw that he was being shot, Hansford began to rise from the chair and move to Williams' right, towards the exit from the room. As he moved, fatally shot in the heart (aorta), he brought his hands to his chest, turned, and fell face-down on the floor along the length of the desk. In his rising and falling, Hansford knocked over the chair. Williams then walked around or leaned over the desk and delivered a *coup de grâce* to the head and the back.

"He then put the gun down on the middle of the desk, went into another room, got another Luger, came back and stood at the right-front of the desk—by Hansford's head—and shot at 'himself,' hitting the pile of papers with the buckle in it.

"The bullet tearing into the pile of papers scattered small paper fragments over the gun on the desk (the gun, according to Williams' version, should not have been there when the papers were hit) and lead fragments in the seat of the chair (which, according to his version, should have been obstructed by his body when the papers/buckle were hit).

"Having missed 'himself,' he may have wiped the gun for prints. Then he reached into the bloody space under Hansford's chest and with his finger and thumb around the wrist, pulled the right hand out, smearing the blood on the back of the hand as he did so (while at the same time 'cleaning' the lighter area in the blood under his own finger, at the wrist), and placed the hand flat on the top of the grip of the pistol on the floor.

"Somewhere in here, he called his friend (Goodman) and his lawyer (Duffy).

"And, sometime during the course of contriving the scene in the study, putting things in order for Hansford to appear to have been shot while standing right-front, he placed upright the chair at left-front... but thoughtlessly failed to notice that a leg of the chair had come down on the victim's trouser leg.... Presumably at the same time, he laid the *TV Guide* on the top of the pile of bullet-wounded papers.

"He then set about 'wrecking' the house in the area of the foyer and living room, where he claimed the initial 'attack' and continued 'rampage' occurred. (Testimony and photographs of the entire scene indicate that the more valuable of the damaged items were very 'carefully' broken.)

"This done, he called the police."

Savannah police detectives D. Everette Ragan and Joseph. P. Jordan, as well as Dr. Larry Howard, the head of the state crime lab, testified about the bullet wounds and the position of Danny's body. They explained the prosecution's theory of the shooting and the elements of the death scene that appeared to be staged.

The Gunshots and Gunshot Residue

The key issue in the case was who shot first: Danny or Jim? Jim tried to justify shooting Danny on the basis that Danny shot at him first. What became an important determining factor was the presence or absence of gunshot residue on Danny's hands. If there was gunshot residue was on Danny's hands, it would mean that Danny had fired at Jim—making a reasonable case for self-defense. If no gunshot residue was found on Danny's hands, making the case for self-defense was more complicated.

Det. Joseph P. Jordan was in charge of safeguarding any gunshot residue on Danny's hands and shirt. In accordance with police department procedure, Jordan said he put paper bags on Danny's hands at the death scene before the body was taken to the Candler Hospital morgue. The purpose of bagging the hands at the scene was to protect against any disturbance of residue until swabbings could be taken just before the autopsy, and then sent to the state crime lab for analysis.

This key test got caught up in a backlog of work at the state crime lab and was delayed until June. Fortunately for the prosecution, when the tests came back, they were completely negative for any gunshot powder on Danny's hands and shirt.

During the trial, Spencer Lawton called on Roger Parian from the state crime lab branch in Savannah. Parian testified that the German Luger that Danny allegedly fired did produce significant residue after one shot and even higher levels of residue with additional shots. The state crime lab's expert, Randall Riddell, performed the gunshot residue test. The results were completely negative, which he considered significant. Riddell went on to say that he doubted that Hansford fired the weapon.

Neither German Luger had fingerprints on them, which was not unusual. Det. Jordan explained that the Luger handgrip is too rough to get a good print.

Luger pistol
Photo by Rama

Next, state pathologist Dr. Richard Draffin testified about the three shots that Danny sustained and estimated that he died within 30 seconds of being shot. Draffin said he did not know which shot was the first. One shot entered Danny's chest with a slight downward angle, severing his aorta; another shot entered the right side of his head and caused extensive brain damage; a third wound was in the back. Either the shot to the chest or the shot to the head could by itself have been fatal.

It should be noted that Chatham County has long had a very distinguished and respected coroner, Dr. James Metts, who came to Mercer House about 15 to 20 minutes after the police arrived. Draffin and Metts performed the autopsy together.

Premeditation: The Prosecution's Theory

The centerpiece of the premeditation theory was the early-morning incident on April 3, 1981, a month before Jim shot Danny. Jim called the police, and Cpl. Mike Anderson and his officers went to Mercer House. According to Lawton's case summary: "They arrived to find Williams downstairs pointing out various items of damaged furniture which Williams said Hansford had broken in a rampage during which he had also threatened both himself and Williams, and had fired a pistol both outside and inside the house.

"There was an apparently dismantled German Luger pistol lying in two pieces on a table by the door; Williams said it had broken apart when Hansford threw it down. The pistol smelled of having recently been fired. Williams told the officers that Hansford was upstairs, armed, and probably wouldn't be taken alive.

"The officers proceeded carefully up the stairs, where to their surprise, they found Hansford asleep or passed out on a bed, not armed. When they woke him and he heard the accusations against him, he became belligerent and uncooperative. He appeared to be heavily under the influence. Williams told the officers, according to Cpl. Anderson's report, 'that for some time now the suspect had been on drugs and becomes mentally unstable.' In the bedroom, also according to the report, they 'found a bullet marking in the floor.'

"Williams said he wanted to prosecute. The officers arrested Hansford. Later that day, when Williams declined to prosecute him, Hansford was released from jail."

Lawton believed that the incident was a staged hoax. The rationale for calling police to Mercer House a month before the shooting was to establish a police record of Danny, high on drugs and alcohol, allegedly going on a destructive rampage, together with and wildly firing one of Jim's pistols into the floor and outside in Monterey Square. Also, Danny was either sleeping or passed out, but when awakened and asked about the incident, he denied it and became angry.

Lawton said that Jim, 51 at the time of the shooting, had characterized the relationship between him and Danny, 21, "generally as that of Henry Higgins to Eliza Doolittle: He had taken Hansford off the street and under his wing, in an effort to 'save him from himself.'" He also characterized Danny "as immature, undependable, and unstable—tormented by feelings of betrayal and rejection—even sporadically violent."

A week later, on April 10, Jim made first-class reservations for Danny and himself on a Delta Airlines flight to London and then on to Geneva, departing May 3.

Lawton found it curious that a week after the April 3 episode, Jim had made reservations for himself and Danny to go to Europe. Jim's reason for having a companion on the trip was his hypoglycemia, which had led to fainting spells. Lawton reasoned that Danny had demonstrated himself to be an unreliable and unlikely choice for a companion entrusted with Jim's health.

The Defense

Cook opened with his star witness, Dr. Joseph Burton, the highly respected medical examiner from Atlanta's DeKalb and Cobb Counties. Burton was one of the few qualified forensic pathologists in Georgia at that time. As a medical examiner, he had performed 7,000 autopsies and certified approximately 15,000 deaths.

Dr. Joseph L. Burton
Courtesey of Dr. Burton

Considering the huge importance of the gunshot residue issue, Cook asked Burton, "If... the hand wipings are taken in the proper method... and sent to the state crime laboratory for analysis and there is a negative result that indicates the nonpresence of any powder residue.... In your professional opinion and based upon your knowledge and background of that test, what significance does that have?"

Burton was clear and emphatic: "It has very little significance to me... A negative test, however, does not mean that the person did or did not fire a weapon. It simply means that that particular test did not pick up the residue that we look for on the hands or on the areas of the body where we might find powder residue.

"It is routine now in the Dade County medical examiner's office not to perform these tests... they are unreliable and we're seeking to find a more accurate test that is more reliable to be used in courtrooms."

Cook reiterated his key question: If all the procedures were performed correctly, would a negative result "indicate in any fashion that the deceased did not fire a weapon?"

Burton answered, "No, sir, it does not, and if it did, a great majority of the cases we now have pending in Atlanta, Georgia, would not be processed."

Cook then asked him if he knew of any experts who disagreed with that opinion.

Burton responded, "I personally do not know of anyone in my specialty of medicine nor in the field of forensic pathology that I consider to be reliable experts who disagree with the statements I have just made."

He also referenced his experience with tests on suicides: of which "Dekalb and Cobb Counties, for the past 10 years, has had one of the highest suicide rates of any county in the entire nation. On all of these cases we have routinely taken swabbings on people who died of gunshot wounds and sent them to the lab and in no single year since 1973 have I had greater than a 50 percent positive return on these tests when the tests are being done by people who are trained to take them, the swabbings, and presently my own technician and myself are taking swabbings to see if we can improve the percentage of positive results from these tests."

Cook asked him about FBI studies of the accuracy of such tests.

Burton replied, "For about seven or eight years in the past, the FBI has kept records of all the tests sent to them for analysis of gunshot residue on the hands. These are tests they have no control over: they do not know who took the tests; how they were taken; they simply receive a kit in the laboratory and they're asked to check it for residue.

"During this period of time, they had less than one 1 percent positive results from the tests sent to them randomly throughout the country." The implication is that the gunshot residue tests on samples from suspected shooters only rarely indicated that they had actually shot a gun.

Next, Cook asked Burton if he had a chance to review the autopsy reports, review the 58 color photos taken at the scene, inspect all the physical evidence at the scene, and make a personal inspection of the house and the room where the shooting took place. Burton said that he had done so.

"When I try to reconstruct what happened at a death scene, I try to not take any bit of evidence out of context, because I can take any one bit of evidence that we find here and make it say anything that I want it to say, but it's much harder to take all the bits of evidence and make them say what you want them to say. However, sometimes they fit together like pieces of a puzzle and can tell us plain as a picture what might have happened to someone.

"We have to understand something about the autopsy findings to begin to understand how this person fell and how he might have gotten in this position.

"One bullet, according to the autopsy findings and the photographs which I examined, struck the deceased in the left upper chest. This bullet did not exit his body, but passed into the body and passed into the lung tissue. Once a bullet passes into the lung it starts to cause bleeding... he begins to blow frothy blood out of the nose and mouth and in two of the photographs... we can see on the left hand of the deceased fine droplets of blood on the back and top of his left hand. These are splatters of blood and on another photograph we can show that on the left collar of this shirt we have the same splatterings that come out through the nose and mouth when someone is shot in the lungs.

"Now, it's also significant that there aren't any other of these splatters around on the floor, on the desk, on the chair, on the wall, indicating that once this person received a lung shot, that the body began to fall and went to the ground and he did not move around...

"With the deceased in front of desk, if he were standing erect, the person on the other side of the desk... firing a weapon at this person and striking him in the left chest, this would be like someone taking their fist and hitting you in the left side of the chest and it would tend to start to rotate your body to the left side.

"It would also cause your body to start to fall.... Now, as the body rotates and falls, it throws the left leg over the right leg. Now the body is off-center, rotated around, and the back of this body is now facing the desk and falling to the ground. The shot in the lungs did not pass through the body, so we don't have any holes in the walls or floor anywhere."

Next on Cook's agenda was to have Burton knock out Lawton's *coup de grâce* theory. Cook asked if he had any opinion on how fast the three shots were fired.

Burton said, "The only way I can make the facts fit the autopsy findings, the facts at the scene, the amount of blood spattering at the scene, the fact that the body does not appear to have made any significant movement, is to have these shots occurring in rapid succession, one right after another.

"This would be in keeping with the body falling to the floor and the person firing the weapon at the body, moving the weapon with the body as it fell and firing."

Cook asked, "Is there any way, in your opinion, that you can place the body of Mr. Hansford on the ground, walk around the desk and fire a shot into his head, and satisfy the physical evidence which existed in this case?"

"I cannot," Burton stated.

Burton then performed a demonstration using a desk, a couple of chairs, and Mr. Moss, an investigator for the defense, who lay down on the floor in the same position as the body. "I first shoot him in the chest," Burton said, "rotate him around to his left side, have him start to fall. As his back comes across the level of the table there, I shoot him in the right side of his back, which he has up to me.

"As he lands on the floor, I shoot him in his head and the head shot goes into the rug. This is bam, bam, bam, fast as the body falls to the floor, and it accounts for the bone, the hair, the holes in the floor and the angles through the body. It accounts for the blood splatters. It accounts for everything that I see in the case except for the chair."

Cook called several witnesses to testify about Danny's violent behavior: Nurse Nina A. Kelly and Dr. Aurel Teodorescu from Georgia Regional Hospital, and Gulfstream airplane mechanic Earl W. LeFevre.

Jim's Testimony

On January 28, Jim began his testimony. Cook directed the questions. He told the court about his humble beginnings, growing up in Gordon, Georgia, his restoration work, and his successful antiques business. The problem was that he focused

too much on his success, his very expensive antiques, his trips to
Europe and England, his wonderful Fabergé collection, Mercer
House, and other things that were important to him. This
recitation of wealth had the effect of distancing him from the
middle-class jurors. His haughty attitude just made matters worse.

He mentioned that he kept loaded Lugers in many rooms of his
house as well as an alarm system because he had been
burglarized twice, once while he was asleep upstairs.

He told the jury how Danny rode up to Mercer House on a
bicycle in 1979, looking for work and how he tried to teach the
young man to be an apprentice in his workshop.

He explained how he loaned Danny the money to buy a used
1967 Camaro which was paid back by deductions from Danny's
part-time earnings.

Jim told the following story: One evening, at a social event, Jim
passed out. Later, doctors told him it was a blood sugar imbalance
called hypoglycemia and an irregular heartbeat that were more
likely to create problems in late afternoon and evening. His doctor
recommended that he have someone check in on him and
accompany him when he traveled. Danny often checked in on him
in the evening and sometimes spent the night in the guest
bedroom.

Jim's health issues are what prompted him to ask Danny to go
with him on his trip to Europe in May, but Danny eventually
decided to back out when he realized he could not take his
marijuana with him. Jim said that he asked Danny to see if Joe
would go instead. When Joe agreed, Jim made the reservations
for Joe and Jim for May 3.

Eventually, Jim got to the events of May 1 and the early
morning of May 2. He described in detail Danny's increasingly
violent behavior that culminated in his death. "As fast as I could
pull the trigger, I shot," Jim said. "I was going to stop him from
killing me... I knew that if I didn't stop him right that second... I
meant to stop him." Danny's behavior that night absolutely

terrified him. "I have never been as afraid in my entire life, Mr. Cook," he said."

Cook asked him about the April 3 incident, in which Danny allegedly went on a destructive rampage in Mercer House, shot one of Jim's Lugers into an upstairs floor, and then went out into Monterey Square and fired the gun. Lawton considered the events of April 3 a hoax that Jim created to make Danny look like a madman. It was the centerpiece of Lawton's premeditation theory. Cook opened the door for Jim to tell his side of the story.

When Lawton cross-examined Jim, he encouraged Jim to describe the relationship he had with Danny. Lawton asked him if he had told a reporter four days after Danny's death, "I was determined to save him from himself." Jim confirmed that the quote was accurate.

"Danny Hansford was suicidal and he had a death wish, which he talked to me about," Jim told Lawton. "He made a comment at Bonaventure Cemetery one afternoon to me, and he said, 'See those small tombstones over there? That's a bunch of poor folks. You see those a little higher? That's just the working folks.'

"And he said, 'You see those big ones over there? That's what I'm gonna get. If I die in Jim Williams' house, I'm going to have one of those.' He said that before he attempted suicide and left a note."

Lawton asked how Danny was paid. He wanted to know if Jim had paid him for any other work other than as a part-time worker in his shop. Jim said, "How do you mean? What other work would there be?"

Lawton clarified, "I'm just asking you. I just want to be sure that I've got it right."

Lawton asked for another clarification about Jim's description of the shooting when he said, "I've never done anything like that in my life." Lawton asked him to explain the statement more fully.

"I've never shot anybody before in my life," Jim explained. "I've never even struck a person with my hand. I'm not a fighting type of person."

"Did you ever become angry with Danny?" Lawton asked.

"I became angry with him, yes," Jim said.

"But you never struck out at him," Lawton continued.

"No," Jim stated. "He would have killed me with his hands."

"And you never struck out at anybody else, for that matter? I mean, when you're angry, that's not your method, I take it."

Jim reiterated, "I said, I've never hit anybody. I'm not the fighter type."

"You wouldn't throw anything at anybody?" Lawton persisted.

Jim finally caught on to where this line of questioning was going. He said,: "One night I played backgammon with a man and beat him seven times straight and the next night he was going to beat me. I watched him cheat two games and the third game he also cheated. He said, 'Are you accusing me of cheating?' and I said, 'No, I'm telling you, you did,' and I took the board and hit him on the head with it... and walked off."

Mercer House parlor
Photo by Jeanne Papy

Lawton's Trap

Lawton eventually laid a trap and Jim walked right into it. Convinced that he did not have to be candid about his sexual relationship with Danny, Jim never brought it up, even when pressed repeatedly by Lawton on the nature of the relationship. He testified that Danny worked for him doing various jobs and that he tried to help him make something of his life. Why he took this position is hard to understand, considering that defense attorney Bobby Lee Cook knew that Lawton was prepared to call witnesses who would testify to the sexual nature of Jim and Danny's relationship.

By the end of the day on Friday, January 29, a good part of the trial had been completed. Doctors from Memorial Medical Center and the Georgia Regional Hospital testified about Danny's mental instability, violent tendencies and attempts at suicide. The defense testimony had concluded. There was one last presentation of evidence—Lawton's rebuttal witnesses and Jim's character witnesses—that would take place Monday before the closing arguments would be given.

Lawton had a real bombshell in his two rebuttal witnesses. One was Danny's best friend, George Hill, who worked for Coastal Marine Energy Service as a tugboat deckhand in Thunderbolt, a town on the Wilmington River. He had known Danny for eight to ten years. Lawton asked him what he knew about Danny's relationship with Jim.

Hill said, "Mr. Williams was giving Danny money when he needed it, bought him a nice car, gave him fine clothes, in exchange for him to go to bed with him... to sleep with him."

Lawton asked how he knew that.

Hill answered, "Me and Danny talked about it a few times. I tried to convince Danny it wasn't a good thing to do. It could mess up his reputation if it got out around town. The last time we talked about it, Danny just told me that he liked the money and everything, that if Mr. Williams wanted to pay him to suck his dick that it was fine with him and we let it go at that. I didn't talk to Danny too much more after that. Danny said he liked the money and the clothes."

Savannah was then and still is a genteel and polite city. The vulgarity of Hill's words must have electrified the jury. One simply did not talk graphically in public about homosexuality.

Lawton asked him if Danny ever told him how he felt about his relationship with Jim.

Hill said, "He wasn't real happy with it, but as he pointed out to me, I had to work all week and I walked around in blue jeans and he don't have to do nothing and he's driving around in a nice car wearing fine clothes and golden jewelry."

Lawton wanted to know if Danny ever told him about disagreements that he had with Jim.

"Well, a few times when I was over there," Hill told the jury, "they had a few small ones, whenever Mr. Williams wouldn't give Danny the money that he wanted. Danny would start a small argument and then we'd leave the house and come back later when he was calmed down and Mr. Williams would apologize for the fight and he'd usually give him what he wanted.

"One time there was—I wasn't there when the argument took place—Danny started dating a girl named Debbie and Mr. Williams wasn't too happy about it and he bought Danny a $400 gold necklace and Danny told me he bought it with the agreement Danny would quit seeing this girl and Danny gave the necklace to Debbie and he took her over to the house with it. Danny talked to me about it later that night and said that Mr. Williams got pretty mad and told him that that was it, he'd have to pack his stuff and leave and Danny was real worried that he'd just lost his meal ticket, you know. He was going to have to give back the car that Mr. Williams had given him and that he wouldn't be getting the money to buy clothes anymore."

"Was it an unusual thing," Lawton asked, "as far as you know, for Mr. Williams to threaten to throw Danny out?"

Hill answered, "No. He's done that a couple of times before, you know, but Danny was real scared this time that he really meant it…. Because of that necklace."

Lawton asked when this had taken place, and Hill told the jury, "This was about two nights before he died.

Recognizing that George Hill had a reputation for violence, Lawton asked him about it.

"Yes, sir," Hill answered. "I used to be an alcoholic and I got in trouble with the law…. I quit drinking. I've got a good job now. I've got my own house and I'm engaged to be married. I've got money in the bank and I've just lately straightened my life up."

During his cross-examination of George Hill, defense attorney Bobby Lee Cook reminded the jury that Hill and Danny attacked Earl LeFevre and his son and later broke down the door in LeFevre's house. He also asked Hill about the 15 street lights he shot out. As Hill tried to deny his guilt, Cook hit him with the documentation.

Then Cook got to the real point he was building up to: "So, from May the 2nd of 1981 until about three weeks ago, you had never told what you have just told to a single living soul…. And who did you talk to on that occasion?

Hill said, "Well, Mrs. Hansford got in touch with me and asked me to please talk to her attorney or one of the district attorneys.

Cook replied, "And she got in touch with you because she told you that she had a lawsuit she had filed and wanted to collect some money and would give you part of it, didn't she?"

Hill refuted Cook's statement emphatically, but Cook's subsequent cross-examination showed Hill to be a witness with significant credibility issues.

Nevertheless, Hill's testimony about Danny's comments just before his death created quite an effect. Judge Oliver instructed the jury to consider Hill's testimony for the limited purpose of motive.

Lawton called his second rebuttal witness. Gregory Kerr, who played backgammon with Jim at Mercer House, mentioned that Danny was a nice-looking young man. Jim, according to Kerr, said, "Yes. He's very good in bed and also, he's well-endowed."

Lawton then asked if Jim had described Danny in any other way.

"Well, he described his physique as being very muscular and strong and just," Kerr replied. "you know, the sex was good."

Lawton questioned Kerr about the drugs Danny took and where he got them.

"I knew Danny wasn't working at this time," Kerr replied. "Mr. Williams had stepped out of the room, and I said, 'Danny, where do you get the money to buy your drugs?' and he said, 'Jim buys all my drugs.'"

Cook objected to "the rankest and purist sort of hearsay," but he was overruled.

Kerr was the man who Jim had hit over the head with the backgammon board for cheating. Defense co-counsel John Wright Jones cross-examined Kerr, showing him to be a witness with credibility problems. However, Kerr's testimony probably helped convince the jury that Jim was not truthful about his relationship with Danny and that Jim would strike back physically if angered.

It was unintentionally ironic that the prominent citizens, including Jim's good friend Carol Freeman, who then came forward to provide character witness for Jim, had not heard the testimony of Hill and Kerr. Their testimony was limited to ascertaining that Jim's reputation was peaceable and that they never knew of any drug activity at Mercer House.

Closing Arguments

Spencer Lawton was on a roll after his controversial rebuttal witnesses. He continued his assault on the defense in his closing arguments. Deeply passionate about his beliefs, he was angry about the death of Danny Hansford at the hands of a man he considered evil, manipulative and exploitive.

"Jim Williams is a man of 50 years of age. He is a man of immense wealth, of obvious sophistication. He lives in an elegant home, travels abroad twice a year. He has many powerful, attractive and influential friends..."

"Danny Hansford was an immature, undereducated, unsophisticated, confused, temperamental young man, preoccupied with feelings of betrayal and rejection, even at the hands of his mother, says Jim Williams. I suggest to you that Danny Hansford was a young man who was a great deal more tragic than evil. Can you not imagine how easily impressed a young man like that would be, living in a house, being friends with a man of Jim Williams' stature?

"Danny Hansford was never someone that Jim Williams really cared for. He was a pawn, nothing more or less than a pawn in a sick little game of manipulation and exploitation. Danny may have thought of himself as a bit of a hustler. Well, he was in way over his head. He was playing for keeps with a pro, and he turned out to be the ultimate loser. I don't think he was a hustler. I think he was being hustled. I think he was what amounts to a prisoner in a comfortable concentration camp, where the torture was not physical but emotional and psychological."

"What happened was an act of murder... The self defense was a cover-up. It did not occur. Thomas Hobbes is often quoted as saying that life is nasty, brutish, and short, and surely it must have seemed so to Danny Hansford during the last fifteen or 20 seconds of his life, while his life was oozing out onto Jim Williams' Persian rug."

Lawton referenced the April 3 incident when Danny allegedly broke up furniture and fired a gun into the floor and into the square. Lawton claimed that this event, occurring almost a month before Danny was shot, was a hoax intended to get a fabricated rampage on the police record, a plot to set up a premeditated murder to look like self-defense.

In his closing, John Wright Jones made an issue out of the Chatham County Coroner, the distinguished Dr. James Metts, not being called to testify. "The district attorney has an obligation to present all the evidence.... The only medical examiner on the scene was not brought in by the state. He was there. He was their investigator, who was not brought in to testify, and the evidence, or the lack of evidence, can create a doubt in your mind.

"He [Metts] was the man that made the report and he was the man that supervised the autopsy.... But for some reason or another, the district attorney chose not to put him on the stand. He's your coroner. He's my coroner. That's his official duty, to investigate homicides. So there must have been some reason for not putting Metts on the stand."

Defense attorney Bobby Lee Cook's closing statement assailed the credibility of Lawton's rebuttal witnesses, Hill and Kerr. He wondered why it was only Emily Bannister, Danny's mother, who could bring them forward. He then went on to emphasize that when a man lives in a community for 31 years and has exceptionally credible witnesses who can attest to his peaceful nature, these witnesses must be taken seriously. The fact that Danny Hansford had a reputation for being a violent person should have been introduced by the state.

Cook reinforced Jones' statements on Dr. Metts' absence from the trial. "In fact, he was the senior investigator upon that scene under Georgia law as being the coroner. He had more experience in crime scene investigation than Ragan and Jordan and myself put together.... If Spencer Lawton had had the slightest idea that Dr. Metts had thought that this crime scene was contrived, he'd have brought him up here in a stretcher, if he'd had to, and there's no other way around it… when Joe Burton said, 'Well, I wasn't looking at Dr. Draffin's [the state pathologist] report; I was looking at Dr. Metts' report,' Spencer Lawton looked like he swallowed a rat."

John Wright Jones, Bobby Lee Cook, Doug Moss, & Jim Williams
Copyright Savannah Morning News

Finally, Cook focused on Jim's right to self-defense in the face of imminent danger. He urged the jury to acquit Jim of any offense.

The jury took about four hours to convict Jim, rejecting options of voluntary manslaughter, as well as the self-defense or acquittal as charged. He was sentenced to life in prison. Lead defense counsel Bobby Lee Cook announced they would appeal the verdict.

www.crimescape.com

Chapter 16

Wait A Minute!

Fortunately for Jim, he did not have to go to prison. Judge George E. Oliver granted him release on a $200,000 bond pending the outcome of his appeal with the Georgia Supreme Court. Not long after the trial was over, Bobby Lee Cook received an anonymous letter with a copy of the full unedited May 2, 1981, police report by Cpl. Anderson that included a summary of the April 3, 1981, incident. The April 3 event was when Danny allegedly destroyed Jim's furniture and shot one of his guns into a bedroom floor and into Monterey Square. Anderson's report became a key part of the appeal that resulted in the reversal of Jim's conviction by the Georgia Supreme Court, which ordered a new trial.

In internal documents for his staff, Spencer Lawton wrote that he provided the defense with everything it requested before the trial. Cpl. Anderson's police report contained "portions which had been whited out to exclude material to which the defense was not entitled under the law:" The complete unedited copy was provided to the judge but not the defense. The copy received by the defense was whited out to show only the defendant's statements to police, which is routine practice. Often police reports provided to defense counsel contain edited information, such as commentary from officers and other witnesses whose privacy is protected.

The following text had been whited out: "We did find a fresh gunshot in the floor and the victim [Hansford] was becoming disorderly. I arrested him…"

During the trial, Cpl. Anderson testified about the April 3 bullet hole. On direct (rebuttal) by the state to Jim's version of the events of April 3, Lawton questioned Anderson.

Q. All right, did Mr. Williams undertake to show you a bullet hole that Danny Hansford was alleged to have put into a floor of any place else in the house?

A. Yes, sir. In the bedroom on the right side, which is the south side of the bed, he pointed out that Mr. Hansford fired a weapon in the floor where the carpet's at. We made close observation of the carpet. There appeared to be a hole in the carpet and as we looked the carpet over, it appeared the bullet did strike the floor.

I could not determine if that was a new type of gunshot or was an old one. To my knowledge if the shot was fired, it would have been trapped into the floor and in the carpet, but we could not locate no bullet.

On cross-examination, defense attorney John Wright Jones questioned Anderson:

Q. And he told you that the suspect had discharged a pistol inside and out of the home; is that true, sir?

A. Yes, sir.

Q. And you found signs of a bullet wound or bullet hole in the rug and in the floor itself on the second floor, did you not, sir?

A. Yes, sir.

According to Lawton, during the trial, in judge's chambers, Cook brought up the possibility of an inconsistency between the police report and Anderson's testimony regarding the "freshness" of a bullet hole found in an upstairs bedroom during the April 3 incident. Lawton answered spontaneously and from memory, saying that no inconsistency had occurred. Lawton suggested that Cook take a look at the unedited police report that was available in Judge Oliver's file, but Cook declined the offer. Later, however, Cook claimed in his appeal that he had been deprived of the report he had been offered in chambers. When asked under oath whether he'd ever had an unedited version of the report, Mr.

Cook—instead of answering directly—said, "I don't know what you mean by an unedited version."

Despite Cook's opportunity to read the unedited police report, the Georgia Supreme Court reversed the conviction, "citing a corruption of the truth-seeking function of the trial process." Later, when the court revisited the issue, it found: "...it is clear that no intentional 'corruption of the truth-seeking function of the trial process by the prosecutor has been established here."

When Lawton proposed in his closing statements that the April 3 incident was a hoax, the testimony about the bullet hole took on increased importance. However, whether the bullet hole was fresh or old was of little consequence. Jim could have made that bullet hole to stage a scene, or Danny could have created it in an angry rampage.

www.crimescape.com

Chapter 17

Second Time Around

In retrospect, despite the vaunted competence of Bobby Lee Cook and John Wright Jones, they were outgunned by the prosecution. From the moment the shooting occurred, Jim expected the police and district attorney would accept his word that he was defending himself. He was angry that he was even accused of a crime. Great damage had been done to his reputation and standing in Savannah society, and Jim was very bitter about it. Now, suddenly in a major reversal of fortune, he was a convicted murderer.

A large part of the problem was Jim himself, who thought he could get away with covering up his sexual relationship with Danny. By pretending that he was a benevolent mentor to a troubled young man, he opened the door to some very damaging testimony from George Hill and Gregory Kerr. Jim's haughty demeanor did nothing to endear him to the jury. His attitude helped Lawton portray him as a cold, exploitive monster who kept his poor, emotionally damaged "boy toy" Danny "a prisoner in a comfortable concentration camp, where the torture was not physical but emotional and psychological."

Emily Bannister's $10 million-plus civil lawsuit against Jim was shelved pending the final outcome of the criminal trial. But, as anyone who paid attention to the O.J. Simpson murder trials knows, even when a person is acquitted in a criminal trial, as O.J. was, the civil trial can exact enormous revenge on the defendant's wealth. It is generally easier to win in a civil trial than in a criminal trial. Recognizing the potential financial disaster that Emily's lawsuit represented, Jim enlisted the very best attorney to represent his interests: Frank "Sonny" Seiler.

Jim was fortunate that Bobby Lee Cook was tied up in a federal trial in Florida and was unable to defend him in the second trial. Seiler is a senior partner at Bouhan, Williams & Levy, the law firm that purchased the elegant Armstrong House from Jim in 1970. It made sense to have Seiler, who was already up to speed on the case because of the civil lawsuit, as the lead counsel. Seiler is a very highly regarded and skilled litigator; in 1972-73, he was the youngest president of the State Bar of Georgia.

At the age of 22, Seiler became a local celebrity on August 10, 1955, when he and his buddy Jack Schaaf got into the Savannah River at East Broad Street and swam 14 miles to Tybee Island. It was very tough going against strong tides that were even rougher due to Hurricane Connie. The incident was an early example of Seiler's tenacity.

He and his wife, Cecilia, were already well-loved in Savannah. They were famous throughout the country for creating the dynasty of English bulldogs that became celebrity mascots for the University of Georgia football team, the Georgia Bulldogs. The Seilers' elite bulldogs, named Uga after the University of Georgia in Athens, are traditionally present at all University of Georgia football games.

The first Uga pup, the grandson of a bulldog that went with the football team when it won the 1943 Rose Bowl game, had been given to the Seilers as a wedding gift in 1955 while they were students at the university. On Sept. 29, 1956, when Seiler was a second-year law student at the university, the newly married couple took the pup to the Sigma Chi house across the street from the stadium. The dog looked outstanding in the attractive clothes that Cecilia had made for him. Without any expectation of what was ahead for them and their dog, the Seilers took the pup into the stadium for the first home game between the Georgia Bulldogs and Florida State. Up in the stands, where everyone could see him, the handsome pure white canine was the center of attention. All around, cameras snapped photos of them, including those of the Associated Press. A star was born.

Dan Magill, the university tennis coach and athletic publicity director, couldn't help but notice. He asked football coach "Wally" Butts to talk to Seiler about bringing Uga to the games, because Mike, the former mascot, had died. At the time, Seiler was earning some extra money working for the coach in the athletic ticket office. Seiler, always an enthusiastic fan of the football team, was happy to have his pet enhance the team's publicity efforts. "Good," Butts told him, "have him at every game." And so, this well-tempered, photogenic pup became Uga I and began the long reign of the Seilers' famous Uga mascots.

In a city suspicious of outsiders, Seiler was one of Savannah's own, unlike Bobby Lee Cook, who was from another part of the state, geographically distant from Savannah. The wisdom of the switch to Sonny Seiler was more than just home-team recognition. Seiler was a stark contrast to Lawton. Lawton, though he had limited courtroom prosecutorial experience, was clever and convincing. Seiler had distinguished himself as an accomplished civil trial litigator, but he was not a criminal defense attorney. The contrast extended to their very different courtroom styles. Lawton was a consistently soft-spoken and passionate prosecutor, while Seiler was a dramatic speaker who could be folksy and friendly in his questions to witnesses or outraged at their answers. Nobody nodded off when Seiler had the floor.

Seiler was assisted by Austin E. Catts and Donald F. Samuel from Garland, Samuel & Loeb, the premier criminal defense firm in Atlanta.

Under Seiler's direction, the second trial was very different from the first. The defense knew which witnesses and arguments would be used by Lawton's team and carefully prepared its expert witnesses to counter them. Seiler knew he had to knock out two of Lawton's key arguments: the lack of gunshot residue on

Danny's hands and the chair that was photographed on top of Danny's pants leg.

Sonny Seiler
Photo by Jeanne Papy

The defense clearly understood that the jurors' views on homosexuality had paramount importance. In the first trial, the defense mistakenly believed that it could prevent the subject of homosexuality from being introduced into the trial. Consequently, the team did not eliminate jurors who may have been biased against gays. Seiler was not going to let that happen again.

The defense was concerned about widespread local knowledge of the case and the fact that Jim had already been convicted of premeditated murder. Recognizing that the media was mounting yet another media circus that could influence the jury, Seiler insisted on sequestering the jury. Several rebellious jurors were angry about possibly having to be away from their families and jobs. Judge Oliver listened to their complaints and then told them to go home and pack for two weeks.

This time, the defense put together a juror questionnaire to help expose potential jurors who were biased about homosexuality. Potential jurors were asked questions like: Would you care if your children were being taught by a homosexual? Would you mind if your minister was homosexual? Should homosexuals be allowed to service in the armed forces? Seiler also wanted them questioned about their opinions on using guns for self-protection and on the use of alcohol and marijuana.

At the insistence of co-counsel Austin Catts and over the objections of Seiler, who was not a believer, they hired professional jury consultants. The very careful juror questioning significantly stretched out the process, with expensive consultants dissecting body language and answers to the lengthy questionnaire. The consultants looked for inconsistencies in the answers that were given and body language that suggested that the prospective juror was not being forthcoming. After the consultants presented their input, Seiler politely ignored much of what they said.

The jury selection process was also delayed when the court had to strike a group of six potential jurors because one of them said that he discussed the trial with a juror from the previous trial. Finally, 12 jurors and two alternates were chosen from the 51 people who made it through the initial winnowing process. The jury was half female and half male.

Second Prosecution Similar to the First Trial

The prosecution's case was very similar to the first trial, where the team secured a conviction. Many of the same witnesses were called, and the testimony was much like what was presented in 1982.

The prosecution's major claim was that Jim staged the scene of the shooting to make it look like self-defense. Lawton used the fact that a chair leg had been moved over Danny's jeans as a visible example of Jim's alleged evidence-tampering. Officer Donna Stevens had taken extensive color photos of the death scene and other parts of Mercer House. Lawton used approximately 20 of her photos in the first trial to support the claim that Jim had moved evidence around.

Seiler discovered that Stevens had taken five rolls of photos. Most of those photos had not been used in the previous trial, nor had they been shown to the defense. Seiler finally got all the photos, started comparing photos of several objects, and found those objects were in different positions. This discovery gave credence to his argument that the investigators had, in fact, been the ones that had moved the evidence.

Seiler called one of the objects "the traveling pouch," a leather bag containing a brass belt buckle, shown on the floor next to a chair in two different places. The photos showed that both the pouch and the chair had been moved. A pink box on top of Jim's desk, as well as other things, had clearly been moved around. Stevens admitted that investigators moved certain things. She said that she took photos before, after, and during the moving of those items, but she testified, "To my knowledge, nothing was altered."

The other prosecution witnesses presented testimony that was successful in the first trial, with a few exceptions.

Randall Riddell, who performed the gunshot residue tests at the state crime lab, admitted under Austin Catts' cross-examination that his statement that Danny probably did not fire the weapon "was not an absolute." There were a number of variables that could affect the tests. For example, if Danny had wiped his hand across his shirt to clutch the wound in his chest, gunshot residue could have been removed from his hands.

Savannah Det. Everette Ragan was a key prosecution witness. Ragan had testified at the previous trial that the evidence showed Jim shot Danny twice when he was face-down on the floor, and that Jim had contrived the scene to make it look like the shooting was self-defense.

Defense lawyers challenged whether Ragan was qualified to provide expert opinions. However, Judge Oliver allowed Ragan, as an expert criminal investigator, to testify about conclusions drawn based on what he found at the scene."

Ragan testified, "We noticed substantial amount of blood here on the wrist of the victim, on the fingers, and the hands of the victim. On closer inspection, you can see that this blood appears to have been smeared in these hands. We looked at the wrist. There's no wound whatsoever... there's no reason for this blood to have appeared on this man's wrist or on his hand, unless, at one time, the hand was... under the victim's body, which was subsequently moved and placed out here."

Over Catts' vigorous objections, Ragan went on to say, "Based on the position of the bullets on the body, the position of the bullet holes in the floor, and at this angle as the bullet went into the carpet, I concluded that the victim was on the floor when these two shots were fired into him."

Then Ragan noted the obvious: the chair over Danny's pants leg could not have been put there by the deceased.

Lawton then asked Ragan to testify about Jim's desk and a series of photographs that focused on various items on the desk top. The detective pointed out where a cigarette had been ground out on the top of the leather-top desk, even though there was an ashtray right beside it.

"Basically what you see here are paper fragments here on top of the desk. You'll see paper torn here and paper that is off the side of this desk that is on top of this drawer here to the right side of the desk," Ragan said as he pointed to the photographs. "You notice a *TV Guide*... sitting on top of these papers... as I pick up this *TV Guide*, you can see additional debris that is here on an envelope here that did not appear to be damaged whatsoever. You will see damage to these papers in here, which led me to conclude that after this paper was damaged here, that this magazine was placed again back on top of it."

Ragan brought the jury's attention to the photograph of the Luger lying on top of the desk. "When you take this close-up photograph on top of this weapon, you can see paper fragments that are sitting on top of this gun, which led to my conclusion that when this paper was damaged, causing these fragments to go here, this other paper here, and paper fragments on the floor behind this desk, the gun was in this position, causing the fragments to be thrown on top of this gun.

Ragan pointed to a photograph of Jim's desk chair. "If you look into the seat of this chair, you will again observe paper fragments and a lead fragment.... I drew my conclusions from the fact that there was no one sitting in this chair when these papers were damaged, causing them to fragment... to land in the seat of this chair."

Lawton brought in a new witness, Dr. George E. Gantner Jr., an expert on crime scenes, to provide independent confirmation of Ragan's theory of the shooting. "In my opinion," Gantner testified, "the shots from the gun on the desk occurred before the shot into the desk. In other words, the gun on the floor, in my opinion, was shot after the other three shots.

Gantner said he based his opinion "on the fact that the paper overlies the gun, for one thing. And secondly, the lack of extensive blood on the weapon on the floor, despite extensive blood on the hand."

Seiler cross-examined the new expert, who admitted that he had never been to the scene; never inspected the bullet holes in the floor or furniture; and never personally viewed the alignment of the shots or the bullet markings on the floor in reference to any position to where the user of the weapon may or may not have been standing. The prosecution didn't tell him about hair and bone that was found in the southwest corner of the room.

The prosecution had sent Gantner approximately 20 photographs out of more than 100 that were taken of the scene. Gantner had not been given sufficient information to provide convincing testimony for the prosecution.

A Much Stronger Defense the Second Time

Much of Jim's testimony was similar to the previous trial, with some important changes. Seiler asked him to explain his relationship with Danny. Jim answered, "I got to know him pretty good. He was a nice fellow. He could be very charming. He could just persuade you about anything in the world he wanted to…. By November, December '79, he had his girlfriend, I had mine. But to me sex is just a natural thing. We'd had sex a few times. Didn't bother me. Didn't bother him. I had my girlfriend, he had his. It was just an occasional thing that happened."

Jim went on to say, "He could be very, very nice… and the next moment, just like that he'd turn on you like a cocked rattlesnake. And you didn't know when it was going to happen, and you didn't have to give him a reason for it to happen."

He gave several examples. After Danny had his stomach pumped, when he had tried to commit suicide, he "tore up Clark Pavilion. Three orderlies—they put him in a steel cot. He bragged to me about this." Later, he told the jury about how Danny and his friend attacked Earl LeFevre and his family; how Danny beat up Robert Croyle, who had been spraying for roaches, and then went after him with a baseball bat; the time when Danny beat up his landlord and threw a chair through his window; and finally his sudden attack on his employee Barry Thomas.

Jim admitted that after the shooting, he moved around several things as he searched for his telephone directory to make the calls to Joe, his attorney, and the police.

Lawton cross-examined Jim about Danny's girlfriend, Debbie. Jim testified that Danny and Debbie spent many nights in his guest bedroom and that he had no reason to be jealous of her. When the gold chain necklace inevitably came up, Jim said that he extended Danny credit for the necklace, much as he had with Danny's car.

Lawton probed the testimony Jim had given on the sexual aspects of his relationship with Danny. Jim responded that Danny "was a hustler on Bull Street selling himself to anybody who wanted to pay for it... He was 22 years old. He was no child... I was going with a very attractive young lady who later went back to North Florida, where she was attending nursing school. Danny was going with Debbie and trying to marry her. This other thing had no mystique to it. It was just something that was natural and normal, and just occasionally."

Lawton continued the probe. "...Are you contending that you, at the age of 50, and him at the age of 20, under those circumstances, that that was in fact a natural and normal thing.

Jim answered, "Mmm-hmm. I was 52 years old, but he had 52 years worth of mileage on him."

The defense team created a model of Jim's study in the courtroom with Jim's furniture and carpet. There was even a replica on Danny's body on the floor. This effort made it much easier for the jury to visualize Dr. Joseph Burton's detailed testimony about gunshot residue.

Seiler added an impressive new expert witness, Dr. Irving C. Stone, who had helped a committee in Congress investigate the assassination of John F. Kennedy. Stone was the head of the Dallas, Texas, Institute for Forensic Sciences. Dr. Larry Howard, the head of the state crime lab, took the two Lugers and Danny's shirt to Dallas for analysis. The Dallas crime lab had sophisticated equipment that the Georgia lab didn't have. When Stone shot the Luger that Danny had under his hand, he found that it had a heavy trigger pull, which made it difficult to fire. When Stone finally got the Luger to fire, it caused the gun to jerk around a great deal, which could explain how Danny missed his shot at Jim and hit the desk instead. Also, the Luger had a round jammed in it when the police put it into evidence. The two casings that were found most likely came from that gun.

When Stone shot the Luger that Jim used, he found it had a light trigger pull, which supported Jim's claim that he shot Danny multiple times in rapid succession.

Using a sophisticated energy dispersive X-ray machine, Stone was able to show that Danny was shot from a distance of 4 or more feet away. Tests did not produce any gunpowder at all on Danny's shirt. These two findings undermined the prosecution's *coup de grâce* theory.

Further testing of Danny's gun didn't consistently produce enough residue to be meaningful.

Stone testified that Danny fired a shot into Jim's desk. Then Jim shot him in the left side of his chest. The force of that shot caused Danny to start to spin toward the floor, catching the other two rapid-fire shots, one in the head and one in the back. These two shots were not when Danny was lying on the floor.

Seiler had another important expert witness, Dr. Charles Petty, the Dallas medical examiner who had participated in the congressional panel that re-examined the John F. Kennedy assassination. Petty testified that the first shot that hit Danny in the left shoulder severed his aorta and injured his spinal cord. He voiced the opinion that Danny fired first and both men were standing when they shot at each other. He told the jury that Jim stayed behind his desk when he shot Danny. Had he fired a shot less than 3 feet from Danny, powder burns would have been on his shirt, but no burns were found.

The chair that was photographed over Danny body, according to Dr. Petty, could have been the result of an involuntary movement on Danny's part.

Seiler followed the technical testimony with a lengthy list of individuals who had experienced Danny's dark side: Barry Thomas, Jim's restoration employee; Earl LeFevre, the Gulfstream

mechanic who was attacked by Danny and George Hill; Robert
Croyle, who sprayed for roaches at Danny's apartment; Nina A.
Kelly, a Georgia Regional Hospital nurse; Steven W. Richardson,
Director of Admissions at Georgia Regional; and Drs. Lester
Haddad, Simon Spiriosa, Patrick Brooks, and Aurel Teodorescu.

As in the previous trial, a number of Jim's friends provided him
with testimony that he was a peaceful man and they had never
witnessed drugs at Mercer House.

Seiler had two surprise witnesses. The first was Vanessa
Blanton, who lived at the corner of Bull Street and East Gordon
Street in an apartment that was across the square from Mercer
House on Monterey Square. She was employed at a café on River
Street that stayed open until 2:30 a.m. She normally had 30
minutes of clean-up after the bar closed. She estimated that in
the early-morning hours of April 3, 1981, she left the café around
3:10 or 3:15 a.m. She drove directly home, straight down
Whitaker and made a left on Gordon.

Vanessa Blanton's apartment building

While she knew of Jim and his restoration of Mercer House, she did not know him, nor had she ever heard of Danny Hansford.

Seiler asked her if anything unusual happened when she got to her house.

Blanton said that she heard a gunshot. "When I arrived at the apartment, I was fortunate enough to find a parking place in front of my apartment, and I was going up the stairs, and I was almost to the top of the front entrance when I heard a gunshot, and I looked over my shoulder towards Mr. Williams' house. It sounded as if it had come in that direction. I looked over there, and there was a young man standing there, holding a gun pointing it up inside the square, towards the trees, and he fired another shot.

"I was watching him, and I don't know if he saw me or not, but he started back up the front entrance to Mr. Williams' house."

Seiler asked her how the man was dressed. She said, "Jeans, T-shirt, like most young men wear."

"Were you afraid," Seiler asked her, "having seen the incident?"

She answered, "Well, I was more concerned, living right there on Bull Street, there's a lot of things that go on in Forsyth Park, you know. It's not unusual to hear something at night... I collected my thoughts for a minute and I thought about calling the police, but I looked out the window, and by then there was a police car there... I was exhausted. I went to bed."

When she heard about the fatal shooting in May, she never really made the connection between the two events. Nobody from the police department or the district attorney's office ever came to ask her if she knew anything about the shooting.

Seiler had contacted her two weeks earlier after he had heard that she told a girl she worked with that she had heard two shots. The story got back to Seiler, who subpoenaed her.

The second surprise witness was Claudina ("Dina") Delk Smith, a homemaker who had worked as a medical secretary and was completing her degree at Armstrong University. She had lived on and off in Savannah for 11 years. However, in the spring of 1981, she lived just outside Atlanta. She and her son came to visit her family and friends for the "Night in Old Savannah" weekend festival on May 1, 1981. They arrived Thursday evening and stayed with her cousin, who lived at 17-A West Gordon Street on the corner of Monterey Square. Her cousin's house was directly across from Mercer House. "Her house was on the corner of the square, not the corner of the street," she explained. "If you walked out of her front door, you would be facing the south side of Mr. Williams' house... the Gordon Street side."

The evening of May 1, they had gone to Johnson Square for the "Night in Old Savannah" celebration with her cousin. They returned to Monterey Square, but then she went out again to visit a friend that lived at the Drayton Arms until 1:30, when she talked to her husband long distance and had a lengthy conversation with her cousin. Afterward, she went out to sit in the square to smoke a cigarette, since her cousin didn't want her to smoke in the house. Shortly afterwards she heard several loud gunshots fired all at once. It seemed to her to be all around, not just in one direction. She told the jury that she just sat there for perhaps 30 minutes. Frozen. Frightened. Finally, she walked back to her cousin's house, which meant walking past Mercer House.

Defense co-counsel Austin Catts asked her if any police cars were around Jim's house at that time. She did not see any police cars and still did not have any idea from what direction the shots had come. When she passed Mercer House, she saw that the lights were on and the front door was standing open, but no one was standing in the doorway. When she got to her cousin's house, she went into her bedroom and found her half-awake. She, too, had heard the loud noises. She talked with her and went to bed. She said she didn't call the police because she wouldn't know what to tell them. She didn't know where the shots came from.

The next morning, she saw a TV news van outside Mercer House and read in the newspaper about a shooting had occurred in the house. She and her son left for the beach that morning and then went to Hinesville to visit relatives. After that, they went home to the Atlanta area. No one from any investigating agency had come to her cousin's home to ask her if she had heard anything in the early-morning hours of May 2.

Mercer House

She came back to live in Savannah. Her cousin introduced her to Jim Williams in early November 1982. She told him what she experienced the year before in Monterey Square and he asked her to speak with his attorney. Subsequently, Doug Moss, an investigator for the defense, interviewed her.

Lawton cross-examined her and asked why she didn't call the police. She said she didn't think there was any value in telling the police she just heard shots. After she told Jim, he put her in touch with his investigator and she didn't think it was necessary to call the police as well.

Seiler ended the defense witnesses with Dr. Henry A. Brandt, a psychiatrist and neurologist with a private practice, who also ran a clinic for the poor at Memorial Hospital one day a week. Dr. Brandt had examined Danny's medical, juvenile, criminal, and Air Force records, plus the evaluations of his probation officers. In Danny's records, two diagnoses were given—unsocialized aggressive behavior with emotional lability [emotional instability] and anti-social personality disorder, which Dr. Brandt said were "tantamount to the same diagnosis. It's been described in medical literature for at least 150 years, but they keep changing the term…. Before that, it was a psychopath, or psychopathic inferiority, sociopath, moral insanity… they're speaking about essentially the same thing."

To clarify for the layman, Seiler asked, "When you say… 'antisocial,' then does that mean more than just not getting along with people at parties?"

"Oh, absolutely," Dr. Brandt answered. "It's a lifelong pattern…. The American Psychiatric Association listed the 12 criteria for the diagnosis. To make the diagnosis, the person would only have to meet three of these criteria…. The first one is truancy…. Another is delinquency, arrested or referred to juvenile court because of behavior… running away from home at least twice…. It's a lifelong pattern that exists… of constantly coming in conflict all the way through with any of the rules, regulations that society, parents, legal systems, any authority figures have set up."

"How can this be treated?" Seiler asked.

"I hate to tell you that there's no treatment," Dr. Brandt said, "because 99 percent of the time the patients themselves feel like they're perfectly justified in what they've done… they never show guilt except to play upon the sympathy of the people who have got them cornered. They can look you straight in the eye and tell you the best lie in the world and convince you absolutely that what they're saying is the truth, and stick to this for a while, and two weeks later, a month later, you find out it was all wrong what they told you. And the unfortunate thing is, invariably they all refuse treatment. They only get into treatment situations because they come into conflict with the law... and send them to juvenile court, then prisons..."

Seiler asked: What would be the effect of introducing dependency on alcohol and marijuana to an antisocial personality?

"Well, you've got three raging illnesses taking place in one person at the same time... and you have a compound impossible situation that anybody could deal with."

Seiler then asked him if a person with an anti-social personality were to consume a quantity of alcohol and marijuana might be expected to become suddenly violent and hostile.

Dr. Brandt replied, "Based upon his life pattern that's existed for 21 years, yes."

Closing Arguments

In his closing, Seiler reminded the jury how sloppy the police investigation was. He emphasized that the death scene was not secure and told the jury that the photos proved that items had been moved around by the crowd that had congregated there. "In they come, one officer after another, and it wasn't just a matter of just coming. It's come and join the party, you see, because you don't have many things like this happening in Savannah, in a historical mansion... and they're all curious."

Also, he said, the police didn't bother to take fingerprints off any of the objects that had been trashed or thrown around, like the highly polished silver tray or the 16th-century grandfather clock, to determine if Danny or Jim had handled them. Nor did the police canvass the neighborhood to see if anyone had witnessed the events of April 3 or May 2, as they usually did in such cases.

Seiler also compared the credentials of his expert witnesses, such as Dr. Stone, Dr. Burton, and Dr. Petty, to old Dr. Larry Howard, whom he characterized as a bureaucrat paid to help the state convict people. Howard, "who never put a foot in Jim

Williams' house" and delivered his "expert" testimony with only 21 photos and an autopsy report to go by.

Lawton told jurors that all the negative information the defense presented about Danny was beside the point. "Danny Hansford is not the one on trial today. Danny Hansford is dead." The prosecutor said he didn't deny that Danny was a violent person, but that he doubted that he was the pathologically violent person the defense witnesses made him out to be. He said, "Rather, what Danny Hansford was is not bad. It's sad, what he was, more than anything else in the world, he was vulnerable. He was caught in the middle, a very unsophisticated, uneducated young man, a street kid who'd been rejected all of his life, and he finds himself surrounded... in this penumbra of sophistication, of wealth, of influence, of luxury... Jim Williams' friend. Well, what kind of friendship? What was the nature of their relationship?

"Now the man that will tell you that a relationship between a 50-year-old man and a 21-year-old boy—a very sophisticated man and a street kid—a sexual relationship at that—that it's natural and normal, just like granola—a man that will tell you that won't always tell you the truth."

Lawton then went on to the key points in his case, including the theory that the April 3 incident was a hoax meant to create a false police record of Danny's erratic and violent behavior. The passionate rhetoric of Lawton's closing in the first trial was gone. Instead, he had his assistant stage a demonstration that appeared to refute Dr. Stone's testimony about the heavy trigger pull on the gun that Danny allegedly used to shoot at Jim. Ms. Kathy Aldridge, a petite woman who weighed about 100 pounds, pointed the unloaded pistol at arm's length and fired it one-handed at the wall. There was no jerking of the muzzle whatsoever.

Seiler had put up a very good fight, far better than Cook's. The addition of strong, credible witnesses like Dr. Irving Stone and Dr. Charles Petty to an impressive witness like Dr. Joseph Burton, made the prosecution witnesses seem weak. Seiler's focus on exposing the record of Danny's violent, psychopathic personality made it harder to recognize the poor, troubled young victim that Lawton successfully created for the previous trial.

Sonny Seiler
(portrait)

By conducting his own investigation, Seiler underscored how unprofessional the police investigation was. By demanding all of the police photos and comparing them, he could prove many different officers at the death scene moved items around. What the police should have been doing, Seiler emphasized, was determine whether Danny's or Jim's fingerprints were on the recently polished silver tray that had been thrown on the floor. Vanessa Blanton's and Dina Smith's testimony underscored the fact that police investigators didn't bother to interview potential witnesses in the neighborhood.

On 5:30 p.m. on Saturday, October 8, 1983, the jury began to deliberate. They had been sequestered since September 27. Six jurors had been very angry about the sequestration from the beginning. They took less than three hours to return a guilty verdict. Judge Oliver, who, like the jury, was tired and cranky, delivered a sentence of life imprisonment.

Jim was taken to the Chatham County jail and placed in a special cell away from the general inmate population. His requests for bond during his appeal were denied while his appeal was pending. While he was housed in the jail, he still conducted his antiques business by routing his business calls through Mercer House.

www.crimescape.com

Chapter 18

Not Again!

On June 11, 1985, the Georgia Supreme Court overturned Jim Williams' second murder conviction and ordered a third trial. One of the reasons it took 21 months for the court to rule on the appeal was the time it took to create transcripts of the many motions, hearings, and the retrial testimony itself. While the transcript from the first trial was less than 1,000 pages, including the closing arguments, the transcript from the retrial testimony alone exploded to more than 1,400 pages, not including the four lengthy closing arguments.

The court overturned Jim's second conviction because the state had improperly introduced evidence—the trigger-pull demonstration—during closing arguments, and Jim's attorneys had no opportunity to rebut the testimony. The court also ruled that Det. Everette Ragan was improperly allowed to testify to conclusions that the jury could have drawn on its own. The first reversal had been unanimous, but this reversal was a 4-to-3 decision. Jim's luck with the Georgia high court was running thin, and his finances were showing the strain. Lawton, however, was in good shape, having been re-elected. Seiler, the man who swam 14 miles in rough waters in 1955, was up for another fight.

After the reversal and 21 months in a substandard county jail, Jim got a $250,000 bond and returned to his beloved Mercer House on July 3, 1985. Much damage had been done to his finances He figured that it cost him over a million dollars to defend himself in the two trials. To post the bond, he had to put up Mercer House as part of the deal.

Heavy local publicity and two murder convictions made jury selection difficult. "I think that Savannah has been pretty much brainwashed against me by the media," Jim said. It became clear that despite the second trial's careful jury selection, he could not get a fair trial in Savannah. Seiler wanted the third trial moved to another city. Despite his concerns that a new venue might turn out to be an ultra-conservative city with an even greater bias against homosexuals, he petitioned the Superior Court for a change of venue. Judge Oliver refused.

The defense team came up with ways to streamline the jury selection without compromising its goals to keep people with biased opinions off the jury. The first day, 200 people filled out a lengthy questionnaire designed as a quick first screen to weed out candidates with unacceptable views. The streamlined process seemed to work, and by May 26, final jurors had been selected and opening arguments scheduled. The defense had learned its lesson about sequestering the jury and did not require it for this trial.

The jury was composed of three men and nine women. One woman was selected as an alternate.

Staleness haunts the third repeat of a trial, except that after the second reversal, prosecution witnesses were more cautious about their testimony. Essentially, they were the same witnesses with the same testimony, and the jury left wondering which experts to believe. In the first two trials, jurors believed the local detectives, supported by the state crime lab staff, over the defense's impressive expert witnesses. The prosecution had no reason to think this bias would change.

The gunshot residue was still the thorniest issue for the defense. While Seiler's experts could rail against the reliability of the gunshot residue tests and show a number of factors that reduced gunshot residue, it was tough to convince the jury to disregard the complete lack of gunshot residue on Danny's hands. The other problem the defense had to resolve was the chair over

Danny's pants leg. Lawton had used the chair as proof that Jim had staged the death scene.

The prosecution began as it had in previous trials with Joe Goodman, a key witness for the timing and activities of the May 2 shooting. Because Joe was the first civilian to arrive, when Seiler cross-examined him, he asked Joe if he had seen a chair straddling Danny's body.

"No, I didn't see a chair," Joe replied. "There was no chair." His testimony about the chair was in stark contrast to the prosecution's photo of the scene with the chair on top of Danny's pants leg, giving more credence to the theory of police moving things at the scene.

As he had done twice before, Lawton called Det. Joseph P. Jordan to the stand to explain the importance of protecting gunshot residue at the death scene by attaching brown-paper evidence bags to the hands of the deceased and securing them with evidence tape.

"The hands are bagged to prevent any foreign substance from accidentally getting on the hands in being moved from the scene to the hospital or a sheet or having a funeral-home person accidentally touching and contaminating the hands or wiping any gunpowder off," Jordan authoritatively told Seiler during cross-examination.

Seiler asked Jordan what time he bagged the hands, but he didn't remember. Nor did he remember whether he had bagged the hands by himself. He also didn't remember the color of the evidence bags or the type of evidence tapes used.

Jordan told Seiler that he removed the evidence bags from Danny's hands and swabbed them before the autopsy. Seiler then asked him if they were the same evidence bags that he had placed on Danny's hands. Jordan said, "I had no reason to think that they wouldn't be."

In what was quickly becoming a dull rehash of two previous trials, Seiler injected a showstopper: He called Marilyn Case, a former assistant head nurse in the emergency room of Candler General Hospital, as a rebuttal witness. He not did have to notify the prosecution that she would be called.

When Seiler asked her about her experience, Case said she had resigned her position as assistant head nurse and took a less-demanding position as a staff nurse in the emergency department so that she had more time to work on her MBA. For four years, she had served as Chatham County Assistant Coroner. If the coroner, Dr. James Metts, was not available, she would go to the site of a death and decide whether the body should be held for autopsy.

She was on duty as the assistant head nurse in the Candler Hospital emergency room at approximately 8 a.m. on May 2, 1981, when Fox & Weeks funeral home employees delivered the body of a gunshot victim who was dead on arrival, referred by the coroner. She prepared a medical record, as she did routinely when a patient or a body came into the emergency room.

Seiler showed her the first page of that record and she testified that it was a true and correct copy of the record she created that morning at the hospital.

She explained that the body was brought in on a Fox & Weeks stretcher. Case said, "One or two employees assisted myself and the two funeral home men to pick up the body on the sheet it was laying on, on their stretcher, and transfer it to one of my stretchers. The coverings that were on top of the body, including the purple funeral-home cover, were returned to the funeral home."

Case said she observed the appearance of the body and read what she had written in her report: "White male via funeral home with multiple gunshot wounds in head and chest. White shoes, gray socks, blue jeans, black belt, and pink striped shirt was left on the body."

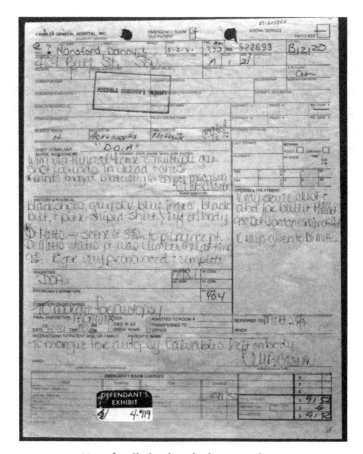

**Hansford's body admittance sheet
(portrait)**

"Dr. Metts was at the scene at 3:45 to pronounce the patient dead. Dr. Metts stated that the patient was limber at that time. At 9:30 a.m., I charted that rigor mortis was very pronounced and complete."

Seiler then spoke: "All right, now, stop right there for me, please, ma'am. Tell this jury, Ms. Case, please, ma'am, whether or not this deceased's hands were bagged when you received him at the hospital."

"No, sir," Case replied, "they were not."

"Now, did you receive any instructions from the coroner concerning the management of the body?" Seiler asked.

"Yes," she said. "Prior to the body coming into the emergency department, Dr. Metts called me, asked me to bag the hands in the department. He also asked me to have the skull, chest, and abdomen x-rayed for bullet placement, and when I was completed with that, I should notify Det. Jordan of the Savannah Police Department."

Reading from her document, she said "I personally, myself, 'bagged the hands bilaterally in the emergency room, per MB Case.'" She used a plastic garbage bag on each hand and wrapped adhesive tape around each bag to secure it to the wrist. She then put a sheet over the body, which was sent to the radiology department for the x-rays Metts had ordered. Once the radiological work was completed, the body was brought back to the emergency room. It stayed there until 12:15 p.m., when it was transported to the morgue to be held for autopsy.

On her record, Case documented that Metts called her. She wrote that she received the body at 7:52 a.m., and she included his instructions about bagging the hands, ordering the x-rays and calling Jordan, which she did at 9:45 a.m. Case showed the jury her written record, including the place where she charted that she personally bagged the hands bilaterally in the emergency room and initialed it.

"Did you ever see or talk to any police officer in connection with this work?" Seiler asked.

"Other than notifying Det. Jordan at 9:45, as I was instructed, that's the only time I had anything to do with the police," she said.

"Where are these records kept at the hospital?" Seiler said.

"In the medical records department," she told him.

"And would it have been available to anyone to see if they had presented the proper authority to see it?" Seiler asked.

"Yes," she answered. She also told him it would have been kept with the autopsy records in one folder.

Case acknowledged she was contacted about this incident for the first time a few days before the trial began, when Seiler visited her along with co-counsel, Don Samuel.

Because six years had passed, she did not immediately remember the incident until she saw her handwriting all over the record, but she had no doubts whatsoever about the accuracy of the report.

Marilyn Case's testimony, which directly contradicted Jordan's testimony on the most critical aspect of the prosecution's case, must have horrified Spencer Lawton. Worse, if her testimony held up, it meant that Lawton's witness had taken the stand and perjured himself in three trials. Unprepared for this surprise, Lawton had to cross-examine her and hope that he could find something to generate doubts about her claims. According to Nancy Amons, who was covering the trial for WTOC in Savannah, Lawton looked flustered and humiliated as he cross-examined Case.

By the end of Case's testimony, the defense had established that Danny's hands had been moved around without bags to protect any gunshot residue while investigators removed his long-sleeve shirt to photograph and assess his wounds at the scene. His bloody body was then wrapped in sheets and funeral-home coverings, and he was loaded onto a stretcher by the funeral-home employees. When they reached Candler Hospital's emergency room, the stretcher was unloaded and the funeral-home employees removed the bloody sheet and wrappings. At the hospital, Danny's body was rewrapped in Candler Hospital sheets and loaded onto the hospital's stretcher—all before his hands were bagged. His hands may have moved around, rubbing against his shirt sleeves, blankets, sheets, and stretchers—potentially rubbing gunpowder off his hands and mixing it with the blood from his wounds.

Spencer Lawton Jr.

When it came time for Atlanta medical examiner Dr. Joseph Burton to testify again about the unreliability of gunshot residue tests, he commented on Marilyn Case's shocking testimony. As an ER nurse, she didn't have the brown paper evidence bags used by the police to bag hands, so she used plastic garbage bags.

"I'd be surprised if there was residue on his hands," Burton said, considering how Danny's hands were handled. Plastic bags are "an absolute no-no" in preserving gunshot residue. Burton also explained that the residue begins to disappear after three hours, and Danny's hands were not swabbed until approximately six hours after they were bagged.

Another defense expert, Dr. Irving Stone, from the Dallas crime laboratory, also testified that he would be surprised if any residue remained on Danny's hands.

Lawton quickly improvised his closing to downplay the now-suspect residue test as only "one piece of evidence among many." Instead, he emphasized the 36 minutes that Jim supposedly had available to stage the destruction of antiques and rearrange the death scene. Then he pointed out that the furniture that was damaged was not very expensive compared with many of the valuable antiques that were readily available to a man on a rampage. He concluded with an emotional note: "What Jim Williams didn't do in those 36 minutes was call for an ambulance. He's been described as a compassionate man who makes contributions to the Humane Society. Well, he didn't even call the Humane Society to come check on Danny Hansford."

Lawton appealed to the jurors to be the conscience of the community. We can't have separate standards just because the defendant is wealthy, he said. Jim Williams killed Danny on a whim. He was tired of him, Lawton told the jury.

Seiler had plenty to say in closing about the quality of the prosecution's case: a grand theory unsupported by the evidence. The investigation was a circus, with cops running all over the house, making coffee, making jokes, moving things around. Too busy to bag Danny's hands and then they lied about it—for six years. Seiler told the jury that Marilyn Case's document destroyed the prosecution's credibility.

The case went to the jury on June 5, but it soon became obvious that they would not reach a unanimous verdict. One woman refused to vote for Jim's guilt. She was the sole person on the jury who had experienced a life-and-death situation not unlike the one Jim described with Danny. When her boyfriend tried to strangle her, she grabbed a kitchen knife and stabbed him severely enough to stop his attack, but did not kill him. She wasn't going to give in to the other 11 people who wanted her to vote against her conscience.

On Tuesday, June 9, 1987, a frustrated and angry Judge Oliver declared a mistrial. Jim was allowed to remain free until the decision after a fourth trial.

Chapter 19

Augusta!

In an interview with Spencer Lawton, I asked him why he insisted on a fourth trial. He gave me several reasons. First, of the 36 jurors in the first three trials, 35 had voted to convict Jim. Lawton believed he owed it to those 35 jurors to pursue the case. With the limited budgetary resources of the prosecutor's office, he had done quite well. He was up against the best southern defense attorneys that money could buy, as well as top-notch expert witnesses and political headwinds at the Georgia Supreme Court.

Yet he had been on track to win three convictions, even with the startling lies under oath by a Savannah detective, if it had not been for the one juror. There was another reason: Lawton, who is very focused on victims' rights, so passionately believed that Jim was guilty of cold-blooded murder that he wanted to see him punished for it. He wanted justice for the emotionally disturbed young man, whom he believed had been exploited by a wealthy manipulator. Jim Williams and some of his supporters were convinced that Lawton was motivated by campaign money donated by Jim's arch rival, Lee Adler. Lawton vigorously denied it.

It would have been nearly impossible to get an impartial jury in Savannah after three high-profile trials. Seiler was able to make a good case for a new venue for the fourth trial. The media had heard that some of the jurors in the third trial had called Jim a "faggot," and said they didn't care if he lived or died.

Mandatory retirement age forced Judge George Oliver to a role of senior judge. He gave way to Chatham County Superior Court Judge James W. Head to preside over the fourth Jim Williams trial.

Judge Head's clerk during the fourth trial, Michael H. Barker, is now Chatham County Magistrate Court Judge. Barker reaffirmed the reason for the change of venue: everyone in Savannah knew about the case.

The choice of city for the fourth Williams trial, Barker said, was basically Judge Head's decision, but he received input from the attorneys. The goal was to find a city with similar demographics so that a comparable jury could be seated. Atlanta was too large, and a city like Tifton was too small. Judge Head chose Augusta because the city came closest to Savannah's size and demographics.

Proceedings began in Augusta on May 1, 1989. Two days later, a jury of six men and women was selected, along with one man and two women as alternates. Trial testimony began May 4, 1989. District Attorney Spencer Lawton Jr. and Chief Assistant District Attorney David Lock presented the prosecution's case. Frank "Sonny" Seiler and Don Samuel presented the defense case.

The Williams case, with its four trials for premeditated murder, was unique in Georgia criminal history. Lawton's three central arguments for the four trials—the creation of a hoax on April 3, 1981, to put Danny on record as a crazed gunman; the staging of the crime scene to look like self-defense; and the lack of gunshot residue on Danny's hands—weakened under increasing scrutiny.

His theory that the April 3 incident was a premeditated hoax was not substantiated with any physical evidence. Several people, including Joe Goodman and Douglas Seyle, said they heard Danny admit going on a destructive rampage. Danny's girlfriend, Debbie, told Lawton's investigator that Danny had described the entire incident to her. More important, a young neighbor, Vanessa Blanton, had witnessed a young man like Danny shooting twice into Monterey Square on April 3.

Police photos of the scene demonstrated that a large contingent of officers milled around the death scene and moving items around. One photo even captured Jim's cat, Sheldon, roaming freely at the scene.

Dr. Larry Howard, the former head of the state crime lab, was inconsistent in key testimony about where Jim was standing when he shot Danny. Expert defense witnesses like Dr. Joseph Burton, the Atlanta medical examiner, Dr. Irving Stone and Dr. Charles Petty of the prestigious Dallas forensics lab, supported Jim's version of the shooting.

The gunshot residue test and the chair placed over Danny pants leg were still major issues for the defense. Seiler had three witnesses who did not see a chair near Danny's body: Joe Goodman, the emergency services technician who examined Danny, and a funeral home employee who transported the body to the hospital.

Before the trial started, Seiler believed that Lawton would try to discredit Marilyn Case's testimony from the third trial that Danny's hands were not bagged at the death scene. He made it his business to find others who could testify to the same information as Case had. Timothy H. Holbrook was one of the men from the Fox & Weeks funeral home who picked up Danny's body and took it to the Candler Hospital emergency room. He said the hands were not bagged when he picked up the body.

Seiler then learned that the first person to write on the Candler Hospital record for Danny was not Marilyn Case, but Angela Douglas, who put the plastic identification bracelet on Danny and filled out the top line on the record sheet with Danny's name. The rest of the sheet was filled out by Marilyn Case. Douglas remembered that his hands were not bagged.

To be on the safe side, Seiler planned to call Coroner James Metts to testify about what he told Case to do.

Interestingly, Lawton called Det. Joseph Jordan to testify about how he had bagged Danny's hands at the scene with brown paper bags and evidence tape. Jordan told the jury that he did the hand-swabbing samples at the hospital before the autopsy.

Seiler challenged Jordan's lie emphatically, but Jordan held his ground. Later in the trial, Seiler put his witnesses—Marilyn Case, Dr. James Metts, Angela Douglas, and Timothy H. Holbrook, the funeral home employee that picked up Danny's body from Mercer House and took it to Candler Hospital emergency room,—on the stand to testify that Danny's hands were not bagged, as Jordan had testified.

There were four closing arguments: Spencer Lawton and David Lock for the prosecution, Frank "Sonny" Seiler and Don Samuel for the defense. All four closing arguments were polished and professional, but Sonny Seiler's stands out as really capturing the angst and frustration of a decade of Jim Williams' trials.

Frank "Sonny" Seiler's Closing Argument

[The transcript of the closing argument had no quotation marks. They have been inserted to clarify paragraphs where more than one speaker is quoted]

"May it please the court and ladies and gentlemen, it befalls my job to wrap this thing up for the defense. I'm going to try not to cover a lot that Don Samuel went over. I know you're worn out with it. Because of the challenge from my friend over here, David Lock, I am going to meticulously review every piece of evidence.

"I'm going to try to help you arrive at a decision. I don't like to lecture from behind this thing [lectern], and I'm not going to do that. I like to feel that I'm talking with you and not to you. I want to give you a road map that I hope will save you some time back there.

"All right, if I'm unfair in any way to these people up here, you correct me back there, but I'm only human and I've been living with this thing for about eight, nine years now. I've forgotten more about this case than I can tell you, and so I'm going to leave some things out.

Sonny Seiler
(portrait)

"And I'm glad you've been taking notes. I hope you'll continue to do so, because if I forget to bring something up that means something to you that's favorable to my client, I want you to do it for me, because that's your job in the jury room. I can't get back up here anymore, ever again. When I sit down, Jim Williams has had his day in court.

"But I have tried to organize this in a way that it will help you to intelligently and carefully consider everything, their side and ours, and arrive at a decision that I hope will liberate this man from what he's been put through by the worst criminal investigation in the history of this state.

"Now, you know already that this case has been tried three times. I can't tell you why we're back here. Wish I could. But I can tell you one thing that you can deduct simply because we're here, and that is that Jim Williams is still in this court before 12 people to be proven guilty beyond a reasonable doubt, and for whatever reasons there have been, they're all gone his way or we wouldn't be here today.

"Now, when I first got involved in this case, I tried to take a very practical approach to it and this is the way I've got to argue it to you. I want to appeal to your reason, to your reasoning ability, to your knowledge. I'm satisfied with every one of you. If there are any of you here that we didn't want on here, we could have struck you, so I'm not one given to emotion, and I'm not going to argue the case like that.

"I want to talk to you about reason, and in order to understand this ridiculous theory that they've come up with, you must ask yourself certain questions to start with, and one of them is: What is the logic of the state's theory? Is it even logical?

"Now let me suggest some things to you in approaching this. You heard what they say about the case. They say he planned it for months. They say that Jim Williams intentionally wanted to kill Danny Hansford.

"Just a few months before this incident happened, this young man who was given to drugs took an overdose, a lethal overdose of pills, that he got out of Mr. Williams' cabinet, 49 of them, and he came in and sat down while Jim Williams was in his study working and said, 'I've just taken a lot of your medicine; I'm going to kill myself.'

"And Jim didn't pay any attention to him, because he just couldn't believe it. And suddenly, after a period of time, he heard some keys hit the ground, and he looked over there. Hansford had rolled out of the chair and he was curled up on his floor in the throngs of death.

"Now, if Jim Williams wanted Danny Hansford dead, he could have walked out of the room, left him right there, never touched him, no act of humanitarianism, and he would have died. How do we know that? Because Dr. Brooks testified under oath that's what would have happened. Now, there's no evidence that Jim

Williams held Danny Hansford down and poured drugs in his mouth.

"That was the makeup of the Danny Hansford that fits into this scenario. That was long before the April incident or the May incident. Jim Williams gets up and calls his personal physician and tells him what happened. Dr. Anton Williams says, 'Call the EMS.' At Jim Williams' bidding, Danny's life was saved. He was taken to Memorial Hospital. His stomach was pumped out.

"Now, this blends in an element here that I find very interesting, because what they've been trying to do is characterize this as some smart, successful, sophisticated man, taking advantage of a lesser person. Well, let's examine that.

"You know, an interesting thing is when you go to a hospital for something like this, they go thoroughly into your background, and in this case, as you heard from the stand, from what Dr. Brooks said, the man's mother was there. And Brooks testified it was also reported that there was a previous suicide attempt and I documented all of this in a chart.

"And also gathering information from any available source, he was described as being a charmer, a person who was able to get his way. He could charm folks into doing things his way. That's Danny Hansford's mother, folks. It sounds to me like if there was any charming being done around here, it may have been Danny Hansford charming Jim Williams.

"He goes on. The only other remarkable things I see in the history and physical was getting a past history from the mother. He was reported to be a breath-holder, a child who would turn blue. I used the term cyanosis, which is the term for turning blue. And occasionally he lost consciousness over it. He had several broken bones. And then, under social history, there was also a note, the fact that he used drugs. He was reported to be a drug abuser.

"Long before April the 3rd, long before May the 2nd, you see a character, humble as it is, whose life is ruined. Jim Williams didn't do anything to provoke any of that. Jim Williams saved this man's life just months before. This is why David Lock wants to tell you that there's no motive involved in this case. Baloney! If you're going to have malice, you've got to have motive.

"Now rationalize with me. Why would Jim Williams tear up his house and shoot into his desk and shoot three times at 2:30 in the morning in his own parlor, on a weekend where it seems like half of Georgia is in Savannah for "Night in Old Savannah," a festivity that goes on into the wee hours of the morning. It's kin to Mardi Gras.

"Knowing that anybody can hear anything or see anything. If he wanted to do Danny Hansford in the way these guys have figured it out, he could have taken him downstairs in the basement of the house, shot him one time in the head, rolled him up in a rug, put it in his car. A million people could have seen the rug getting in the car and nobody would have cared because rugs go in and out of that place all the time. It would have been over. He would have been in the marsh somewhere.

"'Murder, She Wrote!'—'Murder, She Wrote!' hasn't come up with the bizarre things that these people have dreamed up. I mean, this just doesn't make sense, that anybody would plan it just like that. Why would he shoot the desk? Why not shoot into the wall? Why didn't he hurt himself, like they always do when they're going to claim self-defense and nobody's around? There wasn't a scratch on him.

"Does that sound like premeditation to you? How could he have possibly contemplated this scene so that everything fit? How could he anticipate that Dina Smith would be out in the park smoking a cigarette and hear the shots [claps hands four times] and then no other shot?

"Sure, she stayed out there 10 or 15 minutes. It was a beautiful night. She respected her hostess, who didn't like smoking. And when she started to come in, she remembered that the front door [of Mercer House] was open, the light was on. She goes in [to her cousin's home].

"Now, they criticize her because she didn't go chase them down and say what she heard. Isn't it strange that they didn't even make a canvass of the scene to find any of these witnesses? Hey, we found them. I'll put our investigation up against theirs anytime, and I will within the next hour.

"If Jim staged this shooting, why has he historically been so confused over the number of shots that were fired? Why has he always been confused over which side of his head a piece of shrapnel went, as if that matters? This is ridiculous.

"The first thing you've got to ponder and examine is why would anybody, if they're going to contrive a scene, fix a chair like that and leave it? It isn't accidental. If he was going to contrive a scene, he'd walk around and look. I'll tell you how that chair got there in a minute, but these are the things that you need to first examine before you start even attempting to buy this very bizarre set of facts that they got wedded to in 1981 because of a ridiculous investigation.

"Now, follow. Isn't the main question in this case who shot first? Isn't that what it's all about? I think it is, and if you agree with me, nothing comes into play, not one piece of this bizarre evidence, until the state first proves to you beyond a reasonable doubt what Spencer Lawton told you he was going prove the first day of this trial, and that Hansford did not fire the gun. Okay?

"Now, the only way they can do that is with the gun residue test. The gunshot residue test is their case. It is like a house of cards. If it falls, the state's case falls. It is over. Examine this with me. Think about it as I tell you.

"Is the chair indicative of who shot first? Is the paper on the gun indicative of who shot first? Or the blood on the hand? Or whether or not somebody smushed out a cigarette—and they've never proven who smushed it out or when it was smushed out; they just got a picture of it.

"Is any of the trace evidence in the room vital to who shot first? None of this has anything to do with the threshold question, so this is why it is important for you to take up gunshot residue first and this is why they want now to pooh-pooh that test, you see, because two years ago, thank God, we found this document in Candler Hospital.

"So they had wedded themselves to it for four years, through two trials. Suddenly it blew up in their face, and now they don't want to even talk about it and they don't want us to talk about it. So if you find from the first thing you should deliberate, and that is who shot first, that the gunshot residue test is tainted or improperly performed or that somebody lied about it, then end it.

"Spare yourself the misery of having to go through all this scientific stuff that we were forced to do before we found the truth of a gunshot residue test. And if you find that that test was faulty, if you find that that test was improperly performed, if you find that somebody lied about it, then it's you duty to stop the deliberations right then, because there is not only reasonable doubt, that ends their case, because it has been gutted of the only thing that they've got to prove that fact.

"We don't have to prove anything, although we have. The burden is right there and it stays with them throughout this trial. Now, I'm going to get back to the gunshot residue test, but let's go on now at the invitation of Mr. Lock and examine some of these things.

"The time gap. Well, they were going to show you that there was 36 minutes between the shooting and when Mr. Williams called the police. And in order to do that, they bring Joe Goodman to the stand, under oath, as their witness. Okay?

"Well, you see, they get off in the hole to start with, because what they're trying to do is get Joe Goodman to estimate whatever is convenient for them and wipe off everything else. Joe Goodman very fairly told everybody that every time he ever expressed a time, he was estimating. And they were going to show by Joe Goodman that it was 36 minutes. Okay?

"Now, Joe Goodman didn't have a watch. He didn't have a clock that worked. Whenever he glanced at a clock, it was on a Radarange [Amana microwave oven] and he told you that on that Radarange, the sixes and the eights and the zeroes all look the same. He gave them a piece of paper—let me see if I can find it. [Pause.] I'll talk about this, too.

"I can't find the paper. It's in there somewhere. He gave them a paper that's all marked up. It's on a yellow piece of paper, where he estimates all of these times for them: 'about this, approximately that, about this, about this.' They jump on that and they want to start everything on an estimated time of 2:05. Joe Goodman didn't know any times.

"The only thing he did know is that he didn't arrive at Williams' house until Anderson and the police came, and we all know, and it's in their report, which is in evidence, that he got there at 3:00. So what we can do is work backwards from 3:00 to see about when this fatal call would have come.

"Well, he said it took him eight minutes to drive there. You back that off to 2:52. It took him three minutes to dress. You back that off to 2:49. They didn't put on anything but jeans and a T-shirt. 'This is critical,' I said. 'How long did that second call last?'

"He said, 'Just a matter of seconds.' When Jim said, 'I had to shoot Danny.' 'Just a matter of seconds.' I said, 'Give them a minute. Give it to them. Give them a minute.' So you back that off at 2:48. Stop. It isn't but 12 minutes.

"Thirty-six minutes be damned! It's 12 minutes. Then if you want to back it off to the first call, he smoked and they talked. Take 10 minutes away, 2:38. Twenty-two minutes from the first time, when he knew Hansford was alive because he heard him on the phone. You see?

"So if he had turned around then when he hung up the phone and shot Hansford instantly, it's only 22 minutes. But we know that it's only 12. So they get in the hole with Goodman. Now, this is what they really wanted to get out of Joe Goodman, and then they sought to find out, you know, a few other things about him, but the time sequence was why they had to call him.

"So Joe Goodman arrives and Anderson's been called at 2:58. He's just two blocks from Jim's house. He gets there at 3:00. He's got a rookie cop in the car with him named White. I don't know where White's been since these cases have been tried, but I've never met him.

"And coming back up with White is an Officer Chesler, and he's got a rookie cop riding with him named Gibson, and we ain't seen any of those people here. And so this whole entourage goes up, Mr. Williams is at the door, 'come in, the door is open, he's in there.' In walks Anderson and in walks Joe Goodman. There's nobody there to stop Joe Goodman. They walk all the way up to the body and they look down.

"Now comes the chair. 'Mr. Goodman, did you see a chair over that body?' 'No.' 'Did you see a chair resting on the pants leg?' 'No.' 'Did you get right up to the body where you could see it?' 'I was standing right by Anderson.' 'Was it there?' 'If it had been there, I would have seen it.' 'Do you remember seeing a chair dumped over? 'No.' Not I don't remember. 'No,' he said.

"Their witness. 'No.' Anderson. Give me a break. Anderson. Corporal then and still a corporal now. Anderson says, 'I don't remember seeing a chair.' Oh, they wrench him around and finally he says, 'Well, I think I remember seeing the chair, but it wasn't on the pants leg. It was, I think, straddling the body.'

"'Why didn't you put it in your report?' 'Well, you know, it's just not in the report.' 'Don't you put important things in the report? Aren't you supposed to?' 'Sure,' he tells me. Why isn't the chair in any of those reports if it's so big to their case? They've only got a million pictures of it.

"I tried to get in one, Exhibit 69, and they holler and scream and later they put it in themselves. It's Exhibit 12. I wanted to show it to him. 'Did you ever see the chair like this?' 'No.' The first two people in the room, they haven't seen the chair.

"That ain't all. He puts up the EMS man who came to check the body. They get just what they want out of him. The man's dead, as if we didn't know that, you know. Anderson told them that. But they bring the EMS man. I don't criticize them for that. That's procedure.

"Mr. Segal was his name. When they get through with him, I ask him, 'Did you have plenty of room to work around the body?' 'Yeah.' 'Did you have to move anything to get to it?' 'No.' 'Did you have to pick up any chairs, move any tables?' 'No.' He looked at me in bewilderment, like, is this man for real, asking me about chairs and tables?

"They were squirming over here. I heard all this paper shuffling. Never dawned on them to ask Segal was the chair over the pants leg. So the first three witnesses, and there goes the chair. Now do you want to know why they want to use this chair argument?

"They had to give us the picture, you see. And they knew that the minute we saw this that we'd jump on it as a defense, to prove exactly why he hadn't contrived the scene, because nobody'd leave it like that. And so they knew if they were going to give us the pictures, they'd better do what we call backing and filling, that they'd better go back and find some reason to use it themselves.

"The only thing they didn't have was the evidence to support it. So with the first three witnesses, the chair is blown out of the case. Not that it matters, you see, because they haven't proved that Hansford didn't fire that gun yet. But let's go on down at the invitation of Mr. Lock to do all this.

"What about the paper on the gun? Now, here is the absurd part of the case. You talk about 'Murder, She Wrote' and 'Matlock,' or these things that they confect on television, this is bizarre. Now, get this, because I don't think it's been explained.

"They want you to believe that the paper on the gun is there because supposedly after Williams shot into his own desk, before he shot into the desk, he put the weapon down on the desk, then comes back and shoots it. Puff! Up goes the paper and it settles on the pistol. That shows that the pistol had to be there before the shot.

"Does it? Well, let's see. You see, they're willing to grab so many straws that it doesn't make any sense to them when, in their zeal, they want to show that Williams wiped off the weapons and there was no fingerprints on it. But if he picked it up to wipe it off and there's no fingerprints on it, there goes the paper argument.

"They can't have it both ways. I mean, everybody said they didn't expect to get fingerprints off the gun anyway, but the absurdity of it all, they argue the paper on the gun and right behind that they come, not thinking, just sure, anything, anything that looks funny, we'll put up.

"They don't think it out, because if he's going to pick it up to wipe it off, there goes the paper. So if you want to leave the paper on, then forget the fingerprinting. They can't have it both ways. It's absolutely ridiculous how they failed to connect any of this.

"Interesting thing about this paper. You've got some in the bag. I couldn't open it in here. I can't do a test for you right here. I can't show you. The law won't let me. But guess what? You can. And I can help you do it. I want you to do something for me. They ain't going to like this, but you can do it. It's in evidence.

"Take out some of these paper particles that are so minute that I doubt you can find them. Put them down on the table and take a book. Take one of these things, anything, and drop it near it. Drop it near it. Just put it down. Or just get back and do that one time and see where that paper goes.

"They had so many people in that room over the time of this investigation that they can't count them. And they want to send my man up for paper being on a gun? Baloney! They come in with all this 'Did you secure the scene,' all these glib clichés they talk about.

"'Did you secure the scene?' 'I secured the scene.' 'What did you do?' 'I stationed Officer White at the door.' Rookie cop. 'I said, "Who'd you put at the back door?"' Anderson, 'well, nobody.' In they come, out they go, EMS, coroner, coroner's assistant, Gibson—I mean Goodman, all these police, in and out.

"You want to know how that chair got up there? They knocked it over in the midst of all that and somebody just uprighted it. Or at best—and they wouldn't tell you this, but it shows in the picture, I think some do—that thing's got rollers on it. It's made to move as easy as pie. It's a big old heavy chair. You just hit it like that and the chair moves.

"And they want to—they want you to believe that they had some sacred veil over this stuff when they took these pictures. Oh, is that so? Let's see. You've got a set of these pictures here. Look. Here's one guy. I don't know who that is, doesn't matter, he's in the room. Here's a foot, looks to me like the officer's shoe.

"Same shoe there. Who's this dude in the suedes? What's he doing in there if it's so sacred? They don't even know who that is. Here's somebody else, obviously an officer in uniform because he's got those shiny military-type shoes. Here's this guy again standing there. I think this is a copy. And then you get down, look at this laid back soul. He's got moccasins on. He's right in there with the evidence.

"And they tell you they secured the scene, want you to believe that this girl went in there and took all these sacred pictures, that they want to convict my man. Secured the scene? Crime investigation? Huh! What about Sheldon Williams? Do you know who Sheldon Williams is? He's the cat that's in this picture, 102. You wouldn't see him if you didn't look hard, but there's old Sheldon walking here among the evidence. There's Sheldon.

State vs. James A. Williams
Murder
Acquitted May 12, 1989
Augusta, Georgia

DEFENDANT'S
EXHIBIT

THE CAT DID IT!

Sheldon Williams, the cat at the crime scene

"Now, I'm not going to tell you that Sheldon jumped up on that desk and disturbed those particles, but he could have. What I'm telling you is that good police investigation would have required them to get the cat out of the house and eliminate that. And there's the cat walking among all that stuff. And they tell you they want you to convict because there's paper on the gun? It is absolutely absurd, folks.

"Bullet fragment on the chair? Mr. Lock wants that talked about. Well, look, Jim Williams has never ever said, nor have they proven otherwise, that he was in that chair. He was standing. If he hadn't been standing, he couldn't lean over and shoot the way their own Larry Howard says.

"So what, there's some fragment in the chair. That doesn't conflict with anything we've ever said and they can't tie it up, so let's get away from fragment in the chair. That never has been involved.

"Blood on the hands? Why? Why is there blood on the hands? Well, we know that some got on the back of his hand because, like their own witness said, when he got shot in the chest, he grabbed his chest, turns around counterclockwise, feet twist, he falls to the ground, in a last conscious effort to put his hand out to break his fall.

He doesn't end up grabbing it [the gun] like that, like a layman would expect to rig a scene with. You and I would probably think that, you know, if you gonna rig a scene, you ought to put the gun in the hand like you see on TV.

"All of the experts, including theirs, here's Ragan's been doing this stuff for 16 years, he says only three times has he ever found a hand clutching the weapon. All the other times, the hand's either on the weapon, partially on the weapon, or away from the weapon.

"Now, blood on the hands? There's no evidence at the scene that there was any blood on the palm of the hand. None. The only evidence that they've got of blood on the hand is in the picture, and if they're telling the truth—and you see, they'd like to wiggle out of this, but they can't, because they can't tell you we lifted the hand and looked, because they've already told for eight years that we didn't touch the hand at the scene, even though—even though the pulse was taken by how many people? Count them.

"But nobody ever rolled the hand over to describe any blood on the palms of the hand. The only place you get that is from [state pathologist Dr. Richard] Draffin's autopsy report. But you see, Draffin didn't know that the hands weren't bagged when Hansford was brought there and that the undertaker people had plopped the naked hands over the chest that was full of blood.

"So God knows how much blood was on the hands. We know how it got there now. It got there because they never bagged the hands and the hands were wrapped up in a bloody sheet. So forget blood. You can't send anybody to the penitentiary on blood on the hands, because they caused it.

"Here's one for you. Cigarette smushed on the desk. They have always loved that picture. They've never proved who did it. They said Hansford did it. Who? Who from this stand ever testified Hansford smushed that out? They don't know that.

"They don't know that that's Hansford's pot. It ain't Jim Williams', because Jim Williams abhors drugs, doesn't like 'em, wouldn't take him to London over it, never uses them, wouldn't even take the pills that the doctor gave him, and he doesn't drink.

"And through all these scenarios, not one person has ever said that Jim Williams was drinking or that he was drunk or he was taking dope. In fact, the evidence is to the contrary. He wouldn't take him to London because he knew he couldn't trust him not to take pot.

"But getting back to the cigarette on the desk, it amused them so much, until finally, poor Dave [Lock], in his zeal to just get you to cling to anything, he says suddenly, 'that's why he shot him.' Danny smushed out the cigarette on his desk. Smushed it out. Burned a hole. That made Jim mad, so Jim shoots him.

"What happens to the theory that Jim confected this scene months before? They're willing to, for that one moment, say forget that argument and buy the cigarette. Here, this is what caused it. Isn't that ridiculous? Are you believing these people? Give me a break.

"Well, let's go. I know they want to hear this again. Now let's look at that. That should be up here. It should be above this, not down here. This is the one they don't want to talk about. Before I get to this, let's go back and examine what Jim told them happened that night.

"Now, he's testified in four trials. They've got volumes and volumes of what he's always said about this. He has never ever changed one sentence of describing what took place that night that matters. Never. You didn't see them one time grab any transcript and confront him about anything that makes a difference.

"I thought he did pretty darn good. I don't know how I'd stand up to that, because let me tell you something, let me tell you how unfair and how unrealistic it is for him to cross-examine Jim Williams on what took place within seconds.

"Unless you have been there and been shot at by somebody, when you knew they were shooting at you, you don't know the feeling. And it's impossible for me to describe it, because fortunately for me, I haven't been in that position. Hope I never am. But I've heard people describe it.

"I heard one lady describe it as the feeling you get when you see an animal run over, where everything just goes like that. I heard another person—we've got a lot of cockroaches in Savannah, those big flying kind, jump out of palmetto trees—I heard somebody say, 'it's like a roach that jumps on your bosom or shoulder and you just—get him away.'

"Now, how much would you know or remember after that? And they want him to tell everything that happened. I haven't been shot at. But if I've got a gun available, I'd do the same thing. Anybody—any of you'd do if you get shot at.

"This boy comes around the thing [points to desk in photo], tries to fire it one time and throws a round out, gives Jim time to stand up and get his gun. By that time, he's shot. What does he hit? Hits this [Jim's desk]. What do you think this sounds like when it gets hit with a bullet? Look what it did.

"So Jim hears that. Then he hears it hit behind him on the wall. He hears, I don't know how many sounds, and they want to belittle him because he said he got shot at three times, one time. Who would know? The point is, he got shot at.

"And the other point is that he got his weapon, thank God, and he shot, and he doesn't know how many times he shot. And that's not important. Fortunately, the first one found its mark. All you've got to do is pull the trigger. Bam! Bam! Bam! Just what the girl [Claudina Smith] heard in the park, and it's over.

"Now what do you do? You're scared to death. You tremble. You've got nobody to turn to. There's no roommate, no mama, no relative in the house. He's got to make some calls. He calls Joe Goodman, 'cause he knows his number. And he knows he needs a lawyer. Anybody would know that.

"Well, you see, Jim has never been in any trouble before, so he didn't have a number readily available for a lawyer. Bob Duffy handled a real-estate closing for him. He has to find Bob Duffy's number. He's moving things on the desk as fast as he can to find a lawyer's number.

"Paper on the gun? It's a wonder it's not all over the place. I'd have been digging in there like a rabbit. He finds the number. He calls Bob Duffy. Talks to Bob Duffy for five or six minutes, who says, 'call the police.' He calls the police. Police come, open the house. 'Had to shoot him.'

"'I had to shoot him,' is what he told Anderson, who sat on that stand and looked you in the eye and lied, knowing it was in his report. Wouldn't even give him the break then. I know the court got a little provoked with me and I don't blame the court for doing that, because it took me a long time to find it and to get to the point, but here's what it's all about.

"You know, all these guys, they all make these official reports. Oh, they make them. They make it to the major and to the lieutenant and this one blesses it and this one has to supervise it, this one approves it. Look here what he says. I said, 'Didn't my man tell you that was being shot at, that he had to shoot?'

"He [Anderson] sat on that stand and denied it and denied it and denied it and I tried to get him to read it in his report and he wouldn't read it. Mr. Williams was making an oral argument to Corporal Chesler—another police officer that they never brought in here—free and voluntary, and I walked up and heard, 'He was shooting at me and I shot him'

"Corporal Anderson, Sergeant Izzo, and it goes to the major. And he would deny Jim Williams that. The reason that's important is because if Jim Williams had made an admission or confession, they'd have it up here blown up twice this size to convict him. But when he makes a statement before he's had time to think or deliberate or anything, when it's the freshest and purest, then they don't want to give him the benefit of it before this court.

"Now let's see how truthful Anderson is. Don't forget, they've got more chiefs than they've got Indians. That's another thing wrong with this. The first time, Anderson's in charge of the investigation, he puts White there to mind the scene.

"Then in comes Officer Stevens with her camera, the ID person, who didn't even take fingerprints to see whether my man's telling the truth about Hansford dumping over the clock or the silver tray, and I'll get to that in a minute. Now she's in charge, so Anderson reports to her and she does all these things.

"Then about 3:30, in comes, moseying in, is Ragan and his sidekick, Jordan, and we're going to talk about him some more. They don't get there until 3:30. They told Joe Goodman that they'd been doing work in a bar, surveillance work in a bar. They say they were home and picked up one another. It doesn't matter, just another conflict.

"So when Ragan gets there, Anderson has to report to Ragan. What does Anderson tell Ragan about it? Let's see. Here's Ragan's report. D.E. Ragan. Supervisor, Sergeant Pendergraph. And if you'll remember, the top of it shows that it went to Jim Weaver, the major. All this stuff [was] very important, you see.

"According to Williams' oral statement to whom? To whom? Corporal Anderson. 'Victim was identified as Danny Hansford. Had become angry with Williams because he would not take Hansford to London on a business trip. It goes on. Hansford began breaking up furniture and that Hansford produced a weapon and shot at Williams three times.' Anderson tells that to Ragan. On the stand, he doesn't tell it to anybody, and on his own report, it shows he said he got it from Chesler. Classy investigation, isn't it? Please. Can't believe it.

"Now, all the evidence is gone. We've talked about it all except one thing. For four years, they've whipped us with this gunshot residue test. And Irving Stone, true to his expertise, kept telling us, 'something about it, something about it, I need to know. I would like to know who all handled that body and how much, because even if the bags—even if the hands were properly bagged, if they are bumped around and dropped around from one place to another in the hospital, it's going to knock off this miniscule dust that takes a microscope to see'—that they were going to use to convict Mr. Williams of murder with.

"The same gunshot residue test that was so important that they wouldn't even try to indict him until they got the results. You want to hoot? Look at Exhibit 110 when you get back there. This is the letter from Randy Riddell to Roger Parian dated June 9, 1981, where he says, 'enclosed are hand swabbings made at the Savannah Lab using five percent nitric acid solution and taken of my hands by Detective Jordan of the Savannah Police Department. That's the test. Jordan is the detective who swabbed the victim's, Danny Hansford's hands, at the crime scene,' says Parian. Parian is of the opinion that Jordan did it at the crime scene, where he should have done it.

"And it goes on. 'These tests are being made for your comparison—your requested comparison. The purposes are not intended for the official record. However, if you do not want to report test results, we'll give you the hand swabbing item numbers.' That means if you like it, if it fits into your scheme, we give them numbers and you can use it. If not, let's don't say nothing about it. 'Just let us know. The grand jury hearing is Friday, June the 12th. Detective Ragan would love to hear something from you.'

"Important? You bet your life it was important. It's their case. And we ate it for four years. It was hard to disprove. Why? Because Jordan always historically lied. They'll do that occasionally. The police will lie. And once they lie and get wedded to it, they have to ride it out.

"I don't blame Spencer. These guys inherit this stuff. They have to play the cards the way they're dealt, like I do. But the thing about it is, their investigation ended after seven hours and ours is still going on. Up until the last witness that testified yesterday, I still was looking for stuff.

"Well, what we did after Stone—Dr. Stone suggested that is,— we decided to subpoena Candler's records, see what the hospital had. Not looking for this gem, but looking to find out what orderlies had handled the body and how much and where and when so we could get that evidence to Dr. Stone.

"Well, lo and behold, look what we catch? Keep in mind, Jordan has testified that he bagged the hands at the scene. This is funny, because Ragan sort of shies away at this point. Ragan's okay. He just caught in a trap, too. He shies away. His testimony is, 'I suggested to Jordan that he bag the hands.' Question: 'Did you see him bag them?' 'No. I was elsewhere in the house working.' 'Did you see the body when it left?' 'No.'

"Asked Jordan. 'Did you bag the hands?' 'Yeah.' 'What'd you use?' 'Brown paper bags, evidence bags.' 'What'd you wrap them with?' 'Evidence tape.' 'Show me how you did it.' He holds up his hand right around the wrist. 'You're sure you did that?' 'Yeah. Positive.' 'Why?' 'Because that's procedure. Procedure to do that.'

"'Why didn't you just go ahead and do the hand-wiping test right there? Why wait and transfer him to the hospital? Why not do it right there, like all those witnesses they parade up there with expert opinions said would have been the thing to do?'

"Well, you see, Jordan got by with that for two trials, and we didn't find this until we were choosing the jury for the third trial. We didn't have any time to do anything with it. We didn't have time to find these other people that I brought up here.

"The only person that we got to put on the stand was Marilyn Case, who is probably one of the most credible witnesses that testified at this trial. A very professional lady. And she lets us go out there on Memorial Day two years ago and talk to her. And the minute she saw the chart, she remembered.

"Metts called her, talked to her on the phone. She'd worked for him. She was Assistant Coroner. Told her to get all of this done. She wrote it down. And told her, 'if the hands aren't bagged, bag the hands.' Right there in the hospital. Well, the hands weren't bagged.

"And she told you if they had been bagged—and there are some people that have nursing skills or know something about hospitals—she would have put that. She'd have called the doctor back and said, 'Doctor, the hands are already bagged.' He'd have said okay and she would have noted it on the chart.

"But they weren't bagged. They weren't bagged. So she went and bagged them and she entered it up here over her signature. 'Hands bagged bilaterally in ED,' emergency department, 'per'— *per* means 'by'—'by MB Case, R.N.' She signs it. She didn't document it until she did it because that's the way nurses have to operate. If you document it first, you might forget to do it.

"Okay? Then she calls Jordan and says the body's ready. In the meantime, the body gets carried down to radiology where it's unwrapped again. They make the x-ray, wrap him up again, back to radiology department from the x-ray.

"Then it comes back to the emergency room, and then eventually they carry him off to the morgue, where they unwrap him again and he's got plastic bags that Marilyn put on there after Fox & Weeks brought him, dripping with blood. And they want to put my man in jail with that kind of evidence? You ought to be outraged.

"He goes on to the autopsy. Who's at the autopsy? Draffin, Metts, and Jordan show up. Now, here is the conflict that my brother, David Lock, would not mention that I want to talk about.

Here you've got Jordan under oath for four years that he bagged the hands before they left Williams' house.

"He [Jordan] now says, 'I got to the autopsy and the first thing I did was take the bags off' and do this famous swabbing. 'What'd you do with the bags?' 'I threw 'em away.' 'What'd you do with the tape?' 'I threw it away.' 'Show me on your chart where you bagged the hands. Show me in your record, if it's so important.'

"'If it's this important, show it to me.' 'It's not in my records.' 'Why not?' 'Well, we don't write those things in records.' 'Well, they got a photographer at the autopsy. He takes the pictures they want, two pictures of the body. How come he didn't take any of the hands bagged or hand swabbing?' Because Jordan lied.

"Because Dr. Draffin and Dr. Metts say, 'when we started the autopsy, the hands were still bagged.' So once they take the bags off, if you want to carry it out to its ridiculous end, once they take the bags off, then the hands are so polluted by everything that any test is an absolute null and void deal. And they can't get out of this, see, because it's all their witnesses. Jim Williams wasn't invited to the autopsy, folks, nor were we.

"Well, you see, I can't tell you what happened, but here we are again. Now, in the interim period of time, we go and get Holbrook [the Fox & Weeks funeral home employee]. David Lock wants to know why I didn't put Holbrook up? I'm going to tell him, although I don't like to give trial strategy away. But let me tell you why we didn't call him at the last trial.

"We expected them to do what anybody would do if they had faith and credit in their officer and that's bring him [Jordan] back to the stand after Marilyn Case testified to tell you again—not you, but the other jury—to tell them again, 'I bagged the hands,' and be definite and defiant about it, and if—."

Lawton interrupted, "Your honor, I object to this. If it please the court, he's gone in—he's going into what transpired or did not at previous trials in terms of—."

Seiler said, "All right, sir, I won't cover anymore, but he blamed me for not putting that witness up and I have a right to explain that, sir."

Judge Head instructed the jury to disregard counsel's remarks about the last trial. "I will give you further instructions when I give you full instructions about that. Proceed, counselor."

Seiler continued, "Anyway, I saved him in my pocket to play if I had to play him, but I didn't have to. But he testified at this trial, didn't he?

"Now, let's talk about that, because they say they had a statement from him that said he didn't know anything. Well, let me tell you where we were coming from—oh, here's that thing I was going to tell you about Goodman. You can look at that later. Just remember how it looks, you want to see how he was guessing at time, but we've already talked about that.

"Let's stay on this. So Holbrook, after we interviewed him, I took an affidavit from him under oath. Under oath. He knew who I was, because I told him, and I told him why I wanted him, and we subpoenaed him and that's been testified to.

"They go over there, they don't—see, they scare the devil out of people when they come at you. They don't tell people who they are half the time. And here's what they take from Holbrook, this piece of paper here. It isn't even typed up. Not under oath.

"Holbrook doesn't want to get involved with anybody. He wouldn't have come up here now if I hadn't subpoenaed him. But here's his first consistent statement, when he says they weren't bagged, and he got up there and told you they weren't bagged.

"Now, listen. How does he know they weren't bagged? Because if you ever—no matter how much experience you've had—if you ever pick up a body under those circumstances and both hands are bagged you're going to remember it. He says the hands weren't bagged.

"Well, if you want to say he doesn't remember, that's okay. Why? Because we've got Angela Douglas, and everybody's going to believe Angela Douglas. That little girl won't tell a lie to the world. And they found her.

"But let's don't leave this business about Holbrook. Holbrook said, 'when we got there, there's no furniture around, didn't have to push any chairs out of the way, he was dead, a lot of blood. We put the sheet over him, put his hands across his bosom so they wouldn't flop out and embarrass people when they take him out of the house.'

"Right over the wound. Nothing but blood on both hands. They wrap him up in a sheet like a taco and put another sheet on top of him. And then they put a drape on top of that and off to the hospital he goes for the autopsy that's going to put my man in prison.

"Well, you see, Det. Jordan is still at Thunderbolt [a town on the Wilmington River] on a bond hearing and he hadn't bagged the hands. So when they [Holbrook and another Fox & Weeks employee] get there, they're greeted by this little girl who, Marilyn Case, she already knows he's coming, Metts called her, and she knows what she's to do.

"They get him in the back room, and I'm not being disrespectful of the dead, but they're treating this as a very objective scientific test now. Nurses, hospital people get used to that. Well, they have to unwrap him again. They take all those bloody sheets off of him and give those back to the funeral home and they wrap him up again in new sheets.

"Then Marilyn bags the hands, or maybe she bagged them before she did that. The point is, they weren't bagged en route to the hospital and they were nestled in blood. Whatever gunshot residue may have been on those hands, my friends, was long gone or polluted.

"Dr. Jimmy Metts is their coroner, their official. He got to the scene. You heard him. Extremely truthful man. The first time he's ever testified. Who had to bring him here? Not Spencer Lawton.

Not David Lock. The defense team had to call the coroner of
Chatham County to prove a lie.

"Question: 'Do you recall calling Marilyn Case?' 'Yes.' Called
her that morning after he got back from investigating another
scene on the viaduct. 'What'd you tell her?' 'Told her if the hands
aren't bagged, to bag them, want to do a gunshot residue test.'

"Why? Because he's used to doing those tests because he has
to investigate suicides. The truth of the matter is, Ragan and them
hadn't even thought about it. Metts is the one that thought about
it, and he tells her to bag them. I show him the chart. 'Is this
consistent with all the orders you gave?' 'Yes.' What kind of
person is Marilyn Case?

"See, 'cause they were going to jump her, like [David] Lock did
when he was up here. Oh,... 'she should have put it here [a place
on the hospital form], and because she didn't put it over here,
she's a liar.' Well, she put it here because it was something that
she had to personally do and she signed off on it. It's on the chart
and Jimmy Metts says 'that's exactly what I told her to do.'

"And she is a very proficient, trustworthy, professional person.
Didn't know Jim Williams, didn't know Danny Hansford, and that's
what records are kept for. Flawless. Thank God it was there. But
wait, let's don't stop there. They say it might have been toyed
with. Well, let's see. The next copy went to the coroner, the pink
copy.

"And Dr. Metts told you that when all this flap came up at the
last trial that he was contacted and he went and dug his records
out of the bowels of the courthouse, where they've been stored,
and lo and behold, he matches up the pink sheet to the green
sheet and it is identical. No tampering. Two records. Please, folks,
people are in jail over stuff like this. I had to call the coroner to
get that straightened out.

"All right, it doesn't stop there, because you see, in their quest
to prove Marilyn Case a liar, they send J.D. Smith, my friend over
here, with this record that they get from the court, and he goes

looking for this person whose initials I can't even read. They say
Marilyn didn't know who she was. Well, her name was Morris
then. Her name is Douglas now.

"She is the one who got him first. She filled all this out in her
own handwriting. She doesn't know Jim Williams. She doesn't
know Danny Hansford. She's a clerk doing her job. What was her
job? To initiate this report, because until you got this so they can
write on what's done, you don't go anywhere, dead or alive, in a
hospital. Nurses will tell you all that.

"So she initiates it, she signs it, but what else does she do? She
identifies the body. Where does she put it? Not on the foot. On
the wrist. Now, how many DOAs do you think that little girl's
handled? 'Were the hands bagged?' 'No, they were not bagged.'
She doesn't tell Sonny Seiler that, she tells J.D. Smith that,
because see, they got to her first.

"'Where did you put the ID bracelet?' 'I put it on the arm, on
the hand.' 'Did you have any trouble?' 'No. The hands weren't
bagged.' Well, you see, they had to give us her name. One of the
few things we get out of this deal. So we go to her, but the trial is
over. We didn't get to play her last time. We didn't have the
advantage of her testimony.

"So we not only get her, but we get her husband, because she
says here she is watching the nightly news, the same stuff the
judge tells you not to watch, and she's suddenly aware that her
old friend, Marilyn Case, is on TV testifying about her report, and
she exclaims to her husband, 'that's my report, they're talking
about me. I remember that. The hands weren't bagged. I should
go down and tell them. This means something.'

"I'm not blaming Mr. Douglas for this, but they'd just gotten
married and she needed to work. He could foresee her sitting in
the hall of a courtroom for a long time and so he said, "No, look,
your initials are on there. They found you once, if they want you
they can find you again," so she didn't come down there. We
didn't know about her.

"But after that, when they find her and they give her name, church is out. We got her and we got her husband. We brought them both in here. You heard them. Do you believe her? I think you do. Any need for her to lie? Uh-uh. It's over, folks. No, they don't want to talk about gunshot residue, because that's the only way they can prove that Hansford didn't fire this gun, and they nurtured it with a lie for four years.

"So don't think for one minute that you are hearing the same case that other people heard. You are not. Five new witnesses have been brought before you. Thank God we found them.

"Look, I can't even talk anymore. I've talked enough. You've listened to me very patiently and I appreciate it.

"Good character. Don touched on it. I told you that we were going to put Jim Williams' character in issue. Why? Because a person's who's lived 56 years with no act of violence in his life, never even a brush with the law, not even a DUI, has the right to come with that evidence before you and show you that he is not a violent person.

"He is a peaceful person, and if there is anything in his background, with all the vast computers they've got, they would have had it up there. If he had ever been convicted so much of mistreating an animal, he would have been—they'd have had it. The man's a good man and you're entitled to know it.

"Listen carefully what the judge tells you about good character, because he will tell you, good character alone, good character alone can generate reasonable doubt over and above everything else. Do you think for one minute that these fine people from Savannah—and I know Jim's at a disadvantage because we've got to come up here and try it before you, because you don't know these people.

"But George Patterson, 15 years President, Trust Company of Georgia, retired. President. You heard his testimony. He's not going to stick his neck out on something unless it's true.

"Mrs. Lucille Wright, who everybody in Savannah knows her reputation. Has known Jim for thirty-something years. She's not going to come up here and lie for Jim Williams. Nor is Anne Thornberry, who was born and raised here in Augusta. Nor is the lady from the Humane Society.

"We could have brought a truckload, but that's not going to do any good. Bring enough so you people will know the kind of folks that respect my client, because if there's anything—once we mention his character, if there's anything they've got on him, the door is open, folks, they can bring it in.

"Do you think Jim Williams is a violent man? Jim Williams has a nice family. Jim Williams has adopted a lifestyle that might not conform with ours, but he ain't on trial for that, and I submit to you that the only reason they've ever played those cards is to incur your prejudice. He's a good man. He's a peaceful man. He minds his own business. Does good things. Everybody testified, I would believe him under oath.

"Now, enough. Your duty as jurors. We had 20 strikes. The law gives us that. You saw us use them. You might not have known who we were striking, but I can tell you this: If there's any person on this jury that we weren't satisfied with, if I thought for one minute that you wouldn't live up to your oath, if I thought for one minute any of you had any prejudices that you would hold against my man, you wouldn't be in that box, because they didn't get but 10 strikes.

"It's the only break we get in this thing. We didn't get a break back when it was fingerprint-taking time. They didn't even call for fingerprints on the silver tray or the clock that would have shown, if nothing else, maybe that Danny Hansford's fingerprints weren't on them. See, negative results mean too—they wouldn't give him a break.

"We didn't get to participate in any of that. They could have done all that to see if he was telling the truth. Taken them off the silver tray. I got many a beating for handling silver. They didn't try to get them off. And Jim's cooped up in the back of the house. He can't do anything.

"Let's get back to this. If we had any doubt about your ability to be fair, to put prejudice aside, and approach this case like we had wanted it approached, you wouldn't be on it. So all I can ask you is this: If Jim Williams has been guilty of bad associations, and maybe he has, he's paid for it.

"If he's guilty of a lifestyle that you don't like or we don't cotton to, we have to deal with those people every day. They're part of our community. Some of them are very fine people, some of them are not, just like everybody else. It's a community all unto itself. This is God's world. Don't convict him for that.

"Don't convict him for bad association. He's had enough. He's been punished for eight years over this, because he couldn't get a fair trial. And when we finally proved the lies, we were able to get it up here to you. Be fair. Be organized. Be strong.

"Why did we fight these wars all these years? We fought them for the freedoms that I'm asking you to apply now. Innocent until proven guilty and proof beyond a reasonable doubt. This is why we fought the wars. I'm giving out. I give it to you. We've worked hard on it. Let him go back to his family. He's had enough."

End of Closing Argument

On May 12, the jury began to deliberate. After one hour, Jim was acquitted. The nearly decade-long legal drama was finally over.

According to Spencer Lawton, the quick acquittal occurred for several reasons. Aside from the inevitable staleness of an eight-year-old trial, the Georgia Supreme Court had placed such limitations on the evidence that it was difficult to mount a prosecution as effective as those in the previous trials. Lawton also thought that one of the main reasons for the acquittal was Sonny Seiler's argument: After eight years of hounding Jim, the jury should tell the prosecution to let the man alone, he said. This argument played to the jury's inherent desire to pardon.

**Don Samuel & Sonny Seiler day after acquittal
(portrait)**

I had heard that the jury had only deliberated 15 minutes, but had stayed an hour so that it wouldn't look as though jurors had made too hasty a decision. I asked Judge Michael Barker if it really only took the jury 15 minutes to agree on its verdict. He replied that the total jury time was about 45 minutes, 30 of which were spent looking for Sonny Seiler.

www.crimescape.com

Chapter 20

Some Thoughts on the Shooting

It took four trials, a great deal of investigation on the part of defense attorneys, and a lot of Jim Williams' money to get to the heart of what probably happened in the Williams case. The district attorney's complex case theory was ultimately undermined by a very unprofessional police investigation and perjury on the part of a key police department witness.

I never believed, as Spencer Lawton did, that Jim was guilty of premeditated murder (with malice aforethought, in legal terms). It made no sense. For three decades, Jim had worked relentlessly to make a fortune for himself and to become an important figure in Savannah society. He thoroughly enjoyed living like an aristocrat and deciding who would be favored with an invitation to his famous Christmas parties. The people who came to his parties did not know Danny and would have disapproved if they had been exposed to him. Jim and Danny were rarely seen together in bars and clubs because Danny reflected badly on Jim—the social power broker, the man who met with Jacqueline Onassis, and the man whose home was highlighted in *Architectural Digest*.

Why on earth would Jim create an elaborate hoax of self-defense that would suddenly spotlight his sordid relationship with a male prostitute? If Jim wanted to rid himself of Danny, he had many other alternatives and opportunities that didn't ensure a scandal: He could pay off Danny and change the locks on the doors; he could wait until Danny's next suicidal overdose and not rush him to the hospital, as he did at least once before; or, in desperation, he could take the drug-addicted young man out to the swamps, shoot him, and make him food for alligators.

After numerous interviews and reading trial transcripts, I have come to believe that Jim shot Danny in self-defense. My rationale follows.

In the month before Jim shot Danny, their two-year relationship had approached a crisis stage. Though Jim was aware of Danny's violent episodes with his family and other people in Savannah, Jim had only witnessed it once when Danny suddenly attacked Barry Thomas, who managed Jim's workshop. Jim's personal experience was that when Danny appeared to be losing control of himself, Jim had always been able to calm him down.

Jim got his first taste of an out-of-control Danny on April 3, 1981. Danny went on a rampage, destroying furniture and shooting a pistol into the floor. He then shot into Monterey Square. Jim forgave him the next day and, a few days later, arranged for Danny to go with him to Europe.

Jim's early sexual attraction to Danny appeared to have evolved into an ego-gratifying delusion that he could mentor him. Jim actually believed that he could change Danny's behavior and help him learn a trade. This delusion continued well past the point when Jim should have realized that Danny was unfixable. During Danny's life, many people—psychiatrists, social workers, military counselors, and finally Jim—tried to help Danny, but he didn't want help. He had no real interest in a normal life. Joe Goodman, Jim's longtime friend, understood Danny's character when he warned Jim, "This kid is trouble and he's going to make you sorry someday." Dr. Henry Brandt, the psychiatrist that testified in the second trial, put a label on the problem: Danny was a psychopath and he was always going to be a psychopath. Danny had no true affection for Jim. Jim was a sugar daddy, and Danny was able to manipulate him sexually and emotionally.

Even sophisticated people like Jim, who are master manipulators when it suits them, are not immune to being conned. It was clear to Debbie and to George Hill, Danny's best friend, that Danny mostly had the upper hand with Jim. George Hill said, "Whenever Mr. Williams wouldn't give Danny the money that he wanted, Danny would start a small argument and then we'd leave the house and come back later when he was calmed down and Mr. Williams would apologize for the fight and he'd usually give him what he wanted." Debbie saw Jim behave the same way when Danny wanted something.

Only love or deep affection can explain Jim's behavior towards Danny, which continued until to the hours before Danny's death. Even after Danny conned Jim into buying him the $400 gold chain necklace and then immediately gave it to Debbie, Jim overcame his anger and let Danny come back two days later. One might think that Danny would be on his best behavior if he wanted to keep his "meal ticket," but he wouldn't do that.

Danny complained that because he didn't have a real job, he couldn't get married. Jim gave the problem some thought and suggested a solution. Recognizing that Danny loved computer games, he suggested that Danny go to school to learn about computers. Records showed that at 9:41 p.m., several hours before the fatal shooting, Jim called his computer programmer friend to get the name of a vocational school in the northern part of the state. Jim was willing to help pay the tuition as he had helped several of the craftsmen in his workshop. After that, he further indulged Danny and sat through at least one low-budget zombie movie that Danny wanted to see.

Back at Mercer House, doped and drinking heavily, Danny started to feel sorry for himself for losing the Europe trip to Joe Goodman. He got wild and started breaking things up, and when Jim tried to get to the phone to call the police, Danny grabbed him and threw him up against a door. For the first time, he had attacked Jim, and Jim was scared—too scared to try to call the police.

Instead, Jim tried to defuse Danny's anger. He called Joe to tell him the trip to Europe was off, but it was not enough to get Danny to control his rage. The tables were now permanently turned. Jim, the mentor, became Jim, the hostage of a violent man much more forceful than himself. Once he heard the sounds of Danny breaking up things in the other room, Jim must have opened his desk drawer with the pistol.

When Danny came back in the study with a pistol in his hand, Jim reacted. He testified, "The minute I saw that loaded Luger, I reached in my drawer there, pulled it out, had the gun in my hand coming out. I was coming up from my seated position when a bullet was fired at me. I felt the breeze by my right arm. I'd never been as scared in my life, and I stood up and as fast as I could pull the trigger, I shot."

I have no reason to disbelieve him. I would have done the same thing.

www.crimescape.com

Chapter 21

Aftermath

When Jim regained his freedom in May of 1989, he was in good health and good spirits, even though he was more than $1 million poorer from cost of defending himself in four trials. That December, he held his Christmas party, inviting only the people that had been on his side during his legal ordeals. In January, he started to suffer from bronchitis, and on the evening of January 13, he went to a party even though he felt run-down.

Armstrong House is a rather lonely and spooky place at night when all of the attorneys and staff are gone. Seiler rarely came to the office at night, but the night of January 14, he did. He arrived around 8:30 to check his mail. Then he heard the phone ring outside his office. Initially, he wasn't going to answer it, but the phone kept ringing. It was Douglas Seyle, one of Jim's workers.

"Mr. Seiler," he said," I wish you'd come over here. I think Mr. Jim is dead. He's over in the room where he shot that boy. I'm scared."

Seiler questioned Seyle, who said there had been no break-in, nor was there any indication that Jim had been shot. He told Seyle to stay there until he got to Mercer House. Immediately, Seiler called Jimmy Metts, the coroner, but he wasn't home. Then he called Dr. Tony Heffernan, who promised to get to Mercer House as fast as he could. Finally, he called Walter Hartridge, his partner, and they went to Mercer House together.

They found Jim across the threshold of the door between the study and the front hall, lying on his back, arms crossed on his chest. The lower part of his body was within a foot of where Danny had fallen. He had died earlier that day, probably Sunday morning. Heffernan hypothesized that Jim suffered from congestive heart failure. Perhaps Jim decided to lie down on the floor, feeling weak because of an impending attack. He hoped the pain would pass, but it didn't. The bronchitis had progressed quickly to pneumonia. Jim died at the age of 59, less than a year after being liberated from a decade of legal hell.

Over the years, Jim had told two of his closest friends, Joe Goodman and Doug Seyle, that he was working on a new will, which would give them valuable properties upon his death. Because Jim's death was totally unexpected, it is possible that the new will was never completed. If it had been completed, it was never executed.

Jim made it clear to his friends that he and his sister never got along, but he dearly loved his mother and his two nieces, Amanda and Susan. The only surviving will was dated September 24, 1984, which made his mother, Blanche B. Williams, the primary beneficiary of his wealth. He gave his sister the "sum of ten ($10) dollars and all rights to my papers and writings together with the copyright on 'Psycho Dice,'" a game that Jim devised. Mrs. Williams passed away in 1997 and Jim's sister became executor of his estate.

Dr. Dorothy Kingery
Photo by Jeanne Papy

Jim's sister, Dr. Dorothy Kingery, was not pleased that a book and movie were made about her brother's homosexuality and legal ordeal. However, Jim and author John Berendt had a contract that provided Jim's estate with some portion of the book royalties. The estate did quite well financially from the arrangement. Kingery also netted over $1 million when she engaged Sotheby's to auction off some of Jim's finest treasures, including a set of nine pastel drawings by early American female artist Henrietta Dering Johnston, the ormolu coach fitting from Napoleon's coronation coach, a Spanish-made silver-gilt and turquoise dagger reputedly used in the murder of Rasputin, and a Fabergé document casket presented by Czar Nicholas II to the Shah of Persia around 1899. Dr. Kingery also listed Mercer House with Sotheby's in 1999 at a price of nearly $9 million, but it was eventually taken off the market. Since March of 2004, Mercer House has been open for tours and shopping.

James Arthur Williams' grave

The life of Jim Williams came to a lamentable finish. His unwise relationship with Danny ended catastrophically; his reputation was permanently damaged; his fortune was diminished by a decade of defense against persistent prosecution; his life ended prematurely at age 59; and the sister he disliked was enriched by his financial success. Some said that he deserved this ending because of his crimes. Others believed that he was persecuted because of his sexual orientation. However, because of Jim's tragic story, he will forever be identified with Savannah as its best-known citizen. His legacy includes not only splendid restorations of historic homes, but Savannah's transformation into a tourist mecca.

Photo Index/Credits

All photos not identified as family, victim, by name, etc., are courtesy of C. Elliott Bardsley.

www.crimescape.com

Photo Index Credits

Don Samuel & Sonny Seiterday after acquittal, 173

Dr. Dorothy Kingery, 180

James Arthur Williams, grave, 181

www.crimescape.com

Sources

Books:
Baldwin, William P., Jr., *Plantations of the Low Country* (Greensboro, NC: Legacy Publications, 1985)
Berendt, John, *Midnight in the Garden of Good and Evil* (New York: Random House, 1994)
Cobb, Albert L. *Savannah's Ghosts* (Atglen, PA: Schiffer Publishing, 2007)
Cobblestone Tours, Inc., *Haunted Savannah: The Official Guidebook to Savannah Haunted History Tour* (Savannah, GA: Bonaventure Books, 2005)
DeBolt, Margaret Wayt, *Savannah Spectres and Other Strange Tales* (Norfolk, VA: 1984)
Fancher, Betsy, *Savannah: A Renaissance of the Heart* (Garden City, NY: Doubleday, 1976)
Historic Houses of the South (New York: Simon and Schuster, 1984)
Kingery, Dr. Dorothy Williams, *Savannah's Jim Williams & His Southern Houses* (Savannah, GA: Sheldon Group L.L.C., 1999)
The Lady Chablis, *Hiding My Candy* (New York: Pocket Books, 1996)
Rousseau, David Harland and Julie Collins Rousseau, *Savannah Ghosts: Haunts of the Hostess City, Tales that Still Spook Savannah* (Atglen, PA: Schiffer Publishing, 2006)
Russell, Preston, and Barbara Hines, *Savannah: A History of Her People Since 1733* (Savannah, GA: Frederic C. Beil, Publisher, 1992)
Toledano, Rhoulhac, *The National Trust Guide to Savannah* (Wiley, 1997)
Newspapers:
First Trial: Coverage by Jan Skutch in the following newspapers:

Savannah Morning News, January 26, 1982; January 27, 1982; January 28, 1982; January 29, 1982; January 30, 1982; February 1, 1982; February 2, 1982; February 3, 1982

Second Trial: Coverage by Jan Skutch in the following newspapers:

Savannah Morning News, January 6, 1983

Savannah Evening Press, September 20, 1983; September 21, 1983; September 23, 1983; September 24, 1983; September 26, 1983; September 27, 1983; September 28, 1983; September 29, 1983; September 30, 1983; October 1, 1983; October 3, 1983; October 4, 1983; October 5, 1983; October 6, 1983; October 7, 1983; October 8, 1983; October 10, 1983

Savannah News Press, September 25, 1983; October 2, 1983; October 9, 1983

Third Trial: Coverage by Jan Skutch in the following newspapers:

Savannah Morning News, June 12, 1985; June 14, 1985; June 15, 1985; June 19, 1985; June 20, June 21, 1985; June 29, 1985; July 3, 1985; July 4, 1985; August 6, 1985; February 26, 1986; February 27, 1986; August 13, 1986; September 18, 1986; October 29, 1986; May 18, 1987; May 19, 1987; May 20, 1987; May 21, 1987; May 26, 1987; May 27, 1987; May 28, 1987; May 29, 1987; May 30, 1987; June 2, 1987; June 3, 1987; June 4, 1987; June 5, 1987; June 6, 1987; June 9, 1987; June 10, 1987

Savannah Evening News, June 11, 1985

Fourth Trial: Coverage by Jan Skutch in the following newspapers:

Savannah Morning News, May 3, 1989; May 5, 1989; May 6, 1989; May 9, 1989; May 10, 1989; May 11, 1989; May 12, 1989; May 13, 1989

Apple, R.W. Jr., "'Good and Evil,' but Always Charming," *New York Times*, June 12, 1998

Felty, Dana Clark, "Reclusive Voodoo Priestess of 'Midnight' Fame Dies," *Savannahnow.com*, May 8, 2009

Rozhon, Tracie, "'For Sale' in the Garden of Good and Evil," *New York Times*, June 3, 1999

Mobley, Chuck, "The Book: A Never-Ending Story," *Savannah Morning News*, January 25, 2004

Magazine articles:

Daniell, Rosemary, "The Scandal that Shook Savannah," *US* magazine, May 5, 1986

Downs, Gene, "Mercer House Auction Brings in More than $1 Million," *Coastal Antiques & Art*, November, 2000.

Irvin, Stan: "Bobby Lee Cook Showed Me the Honor in Defense," Cross-Wise With Stan blogspot, April 13, 2009

Miller, Jack, "Savannah: Remembering '69 on the 40th anniversary of Stonewall," *The Gay and Lesbian Review Worldwide*, Sept-Oct., 2009

Stumb, Patricia C., "The Jim Williams Story," *Connect Savannah*, November 26-December 2, 1999

Wilkes, D., "Not Technicalities," *Flagpole Magazine*, March 12, 1997

Documents:

Lawton, Spencer, Jr., "The Other Side of 'Midnight,'" A Fact Sheet

Lawton, Spencer, Jr., *The Williams Case: The History: A Summary*

Williams, Jim, Last Will and Testament, September 24, 1984

Chatham County, Georgia, Superior Court, The State of Georgia vs. James A. Williams, No. 34,982—Murder.

www.crimescape.com